CRITICAL ANTHOLOGIES OF NONFICTION WRITING™

CRITICAL PERSPECTIVES ON THE VIETNAM WAR

Edited by
GILBERT MORALES JR.

THE ROSEN PUBLISHING GROUP, INC.
NEW YORK

Published in 2005 by The Rosen Publishing Group, Inc.
29 East 21st Street, New York, NY 10010

Library of Congress Cataloging-in-Publication Data

Critical perspectives on the Vietnam War / edited by Gilbert
Morales, Jr.—1st ed.
    v. cm.—(Critical anthologies of nonfiction writing)
Includes bibliographical references and index.
Contents: Global connections—Individuals, groups, and
institutions—Culture—Power, authority, and governance—
Time, continuity, and change.
ISBN 1-4042-0063-0 (library binding)
1. Vietnamese Conflict, 1961–1975. [1. Vietnamese Conflict,
1961–1975—Sources.] I. Morales, Gilbert. II. Series.
DS557.7.C75 2005
959.704'3—dc22
                                                    2003026094

Manufactured in the United States of America

On the cover: U.S. soldiers walking through rice paddies in
South Vietnam in 1967.

CONTENTS

INTRODUCTION

As the twenty-first century gets under way, the United States is faced with many difficult geopolitical predicaments in some of the world's most sensitive and strategic hot spots. When standing at this sort of historical crossroads, it is always a good idea to look back and investigate similarly challenging periods of momentous change and conflict, in order to apply their lessons to present circumstances. Traditionally, war has provoked history's greatest crises and ushered in tremendous social and political changes. The many wars and smaller international conflicts that the United States became involved in during the twentieth century serve as a learning platform in which to study our nation's history and development. One such war is the Vietnam War, officially known as the Vietnam conflict, since war was never actually declared on North Vietnam.

The global political climate prior to the Vietnam War was being poisoned by the dangerous Cold War hostility between the Western democracies and the Communist nations of the Soviet bloc. The delicate balance of power between Communist and democratic nations seemed to shift from year to year. Democratic powers, such as the United States, England, and France, struggled to maintain authority and influence in the face of the Soviet Union's and China's attempts to introduce Communism throughout Southeast Asia.

Many argued that waging war in Vietnam was necessary to halt this advancing specter of Communism. Others believed that American involvement in Southeast Asia was unnecessary and simply resulted in millions of American and Vietnamese casualties, billions of dollars wasted, and several nations scarred, both physically and ideologically. There is no doubt the Vietnam War remains the most complicated and controversial episode in American history, one that strikes a deep cautionary note regarding the use of American troops in poorly defined and poorly understood foreign conflicts.

Vietnam, a small country in Southeast Asia, is home to some of the poorest communities on earth. In the nineteenth century, the Vietnamese were colonized by the French in an occupation that lasted until World War II. By then, Ho Chi Minh and his Communist Vietminh party had gained firm control over Vietnam. After Germany brought the French to their knees in 1940, Ho Chi Minh seized the opportunity and declared Vietnam's independence from France. When World War II ended in 1945 with an Allied victory, France returned its attention to Vietnam, hoping to regain control of its former colony. As a result, the First Indochina War exploded in Vietnam.

France, with its superior military, swiftly moved into Vietnam, expecting a quick victory. Instead, France found itself in a war it could not win, as the Vietminh employed guerrilla tactics and used the difficult Vietnamese landscape to confuse and terrorize the French. Ho Chi Minh's forces drove the French to the brink of a humiliating defeat, and by 1954, France had given up. In July of that year, eight countries, including the

United States, China, and the Soviet Union, gathered in Geneva, Switzerland, to work on an agreement to end the war.

While the First Indochina War had been raging, the political fallout from World War II had begun to polarize the United States and the Soviet Union, and their democratic and Communist allies throughout Europe and Asia. An uneasy, heavily armed standoff known as the Cold War resulted, leading to a global arms race and a decades-long struggle for military, economic, and ideological superiority throughout the world. One aspect of this global struggle was the tug-of-war that developed over who would control Vietnam. By the end of the First Indochina War, Vietnam was strongly divided between Ho Chi Minh's Communist loyalists and those Vietnamese in favor of a democratic nation. The Geneva Accords that ended the war called for a cease-fire line drawn at the 17th parallel. The country would be divided into North Vietnam and South Vietnam until nationwide elections would be held in 1956. Seeing that Ho Chi Minh's Communist movement was quickly gaining momentum in Vietnam, the United States made it clear that it would not support nationwide elections. Instead, the United States began to support the creation of an anti-Communist South Vietnam. The seeds of the Vietnam War were now planted.

But the United States overlooked the lessons of recent history—France had just fought a futile jungle war and lost badly. Now it was the United States' turn to underestimate Vietnamese resolve. As the 1960s began and the Cold War escalated, it became clear that the U.S. military was destined to make the same mistakes France had made a decade earlier. Each year, more and more American troops were sent to

Vietnam to support what was now a sharply divided country, a country at war with itself over the competing ideals of democracy and Communism. Vietnam was the cauldron in which the Cold War boiled over.

In America and around the world, the counterculture— mostly young people opposed to the war and government authority—would raise its voice, enlisting millions of increasingly disillusioned young Americans in a long protest march against what was described as the atrocity of Vietnam. Veterans would return home, wounded and maimed, and join the protests against the war. Even so, the war in Vietnam would continue to rage until 1975, when the United States pulled its remaining forces out of Vietnam, and Saigon fell to the Communists.

For the first time in its history, America had lost a war.

As is true of any war, there are many Vietnam stories that need to be told. These stories are far too complex and too far reaching to be fully represented in only one volume. This anthology simply attempts to capture the essence of the Vietnam experience, by giving voice to the wide range of opinions and perspectives engendered by this torturous conflict. Each voice in this anthology is unique—from the desk of President John F. Kennedy, to first-person accounts of firefights in the Vietnam jungle, to former secretary of state Robert S. McNamara's personal memoirs. Unfortunately, no one person has the answers to the enduring riddle of Vietnam. No one person can pass final judgment on this failed American war. Maybe, someday, the history books will provide us with the certainty we seek. Until then, all we have are the questioning voices that, taken together, tell us the story of Vietnam.

CHAPTER ONE

GLOBAL CONNECTIONS ESCALATION, 1961–1965

A Letter from President Kennedy to President Ngo Dinh Diem
December 14, 1961

Signed in 1954, the Geneva Accords theoretically ended the war between French forces and the Vietminh in Laos, Cambodia, and Vietnam. These states were to become fully independent countries, with Vietnam partitioned near the 17th parallel into two states, pending reunification through free elections to be held by July 20, 1956. Even though the United States did not sign on to the accords, it nevertheless declared that it would view any renewal of aggression of any of the parties involved as a threat to international peace and security.

As Communism spread throughout Eastern Europe, America viewed this as a growing threat to Western culture. Many nations in the Western world were wary of South Vietnamese president Ngo Dinh Diem and his despotic regime. Regardless, the U.S. government felt obligated to increase its support of South Vietnam because of the increasing Communist threat.

The following letter shows the extent of President John F. Kennedy's early commitment to stopping Communist aggression in Southeast Asia. Here, the young president is faced with an international crisis and pledges the United States' support in helping South Vietnam defend itself from "outside" aggressors.

———▫———

Dear Mr. President:

I have received your recent letter in which you described so cogently the dangerous condition caused by North Vietnam's efforts to take over your country. The situation in your embattled country is well known to me and to the American people. We have been deeply disturbed by the assault on your country. Our indignation has mounted as the deliberate savagery of the Communist program of assassination, kidnapping, and wanton violence became clear.

Your letter underlines what our own information has convincingly shown—that the campaign of force and terror now being waged against your people and your government is supported and directed from the outside by the authorities at Hanoi. They have thus violated the provisions of the Geneva Accords designed to ensure peace in Vietnam and to which they bound themselves in 1954.

At that time, the United States, although not a party to the Accords, declared that it "would view any renewal of the aggression in violation of the Agreements with grave concern and as seriously threatening international peace and security." We continue to maintain that view.

In accordance with that declaration, and in response to your request, we are prepared to help the Republic of Vietnam to protect its people and to preserve its independence. We shall promptly increase our assistance to your defense effort as well as help relieve the destruction of the floods which you describe. I have already given the orders to get those programs underway.

The United States, like the Republic of Vietnam, remains devoted to the cause of peace and our primary purpose is to help your people maintain their independence. If the Communist authorities in North Vietnam will stop their campaign to destroy the Republic of Vietnam, the measures we are taking to assist your defense efforts will no longer be necessary. We shall seek to persuade the Communists to give up their attempts of force and subversion. In any case, we are confident that the Vietnamese people will preserve their independence and gain the peace and prosperity for which they have fought so hard and so long.

"Vietnam Victory Remote Despite U.S. Aid to Diem"
By Homer Bigart
From the New York Times, July 25, 1962

In the early stages of the Vietnam conflict, it was difficult to anticipate the troubles facing the United States both on the battlefield and at home. However, in this jarringly prescient New York Times *article, acclaimed journalist Homer Bigart casts his doubts on a successful U.S. undertaking in Vietnam.*

Little did he know at the time the extent of the United States'
involvement or how much this campaign would cost in dollars
and American lives. From the beginning of the U.S. involvement,
when the U.S. presence in Vietnam was still considered an
"aid program," not even inquiring reporters like Bigart, let
alone U.S. military officials, could see the obstacles ahead of
them in this increasingly hopeless situation. More than ever,
support for President Diem was quickly disintegrating, both
from within his country and from those nations supporting
him. By 1963, the United States had completely withdrawn
support of Diem. In November of that year, Diem was assassi-
nated, and the situation in Vietnam grew increasingly hopeless.

———□———

The United States, by massive and unqualified support of the
regime of President Ngo Dinh Diem, has helped arrest the
spread of Communist insurgency in South Vietnam. But victory
is remote. The issue remains in doubt because the Vietnamese
President seems incapable of winning the loyalty of his people.

From the strictly military point of view, the situation has
improved. "We are now doing a little better than holding our
own," was the cautious assessment made a few weeks ago by
Maj. Gen. Charles J. Times, chief of the United States Army
element of the Military Assistance and Advisory Group.

However, no decisive turn in the military struggle is
expected this year. The combat effectiveness of the South
Vietnamese has been temporarily weakened by robbing rifle
companies of good officers and noncoms to provide cadres for
two new divisions now being created.

These new divisions will increase the strength of the regular forces to more than 205,000 by the end of this year. In addition, the Civil Guard will be expanded to 72,000 and the Self-Defense Corps to 80,000.

Assuming that the Vietcong (Vietnamese Communist) guerrillas do not receive substantial outside aid, there would seem to be valid reason for optimism. For in 1963 the Republic of South Vietnam will put well-equipped forces totaling more than 350,000 men against 25,000 guerrillas who have no artillery, no anti-aircraft guns, no air power, no trucks, no jeeps, no prime movers, and only basic infantry weapons.

Also by 1963 the Vietnamese armed forces should be adequately staffed with officers and noncoms and be somewhat better trained for fighting in jungles and swamps.

They will have more helicopters, armored personnel carriers and other gadgets to enhance mobility, more sentry dogs to sniff out guerrillas, more plastic boats for the delta region, more American advisers with fresh, new tactical doctrines.

Yet visions of ultimate victory are obscured by the image of a secretive, suspicious, dictatorial regime. American officers are frustrated and irritated by the constant whimsical meddling of the President and his brother, Ngo Dinh Nhu, in the military chain of command.

The President assumes direction of military operations. All major troop movements, all officer promotions, must have his approval. Acting on vague rumors of a coup, Ngo Dinh Nhu last February summoned elements of the Seventh Division to the outskirts of Saigon without notifying the Third Corps commander.

Failure to coordinate with area commanders has also marked the Presidential palace's use of general reserve troops. These have been dispatched on futile one-shot operations based on faulty intelligence and conducted with slipshod planning.

In situations demanding fast action or improvisation, the palace's tight control of the army has killed initiative. In June, guerrillas wiped out a convoy forty miles north of Saigon, killing two American officers. The only soldiers available for pursuit belonged to the general reserve.

Hours elapsed before Presidential consent could be obtained for the employment of these troops, and it was early evening when United States Marine helicopters put them down on the guerrillas' trail. The guerrillas got away easily despite their heavy booty in guns and ammunition.

This episode was a bitter revelation for Americans. The ambush took place on the outskirts of Bentre, a garrison town, and on a heavily traveled highway. Yet the guerrillas moved into position in daylight, prepared the ambuscade in full view of the road and waited three hours for the convoy to appear. They must have been observed by scores of peasants. Yet no one informed the garrison in Bentre.

Could this have happened if peasants felt any real identification with the regime?

A family living at the scene said it was threatened with death if it informed. But the Vietcong probably would never have undertaken this action without full confidence that the peasants were with them, or at least indifferent.

There is no accurate gauge of sentiment in Vietnam. The press is rigidly controlled and there is no freedom of assembly.

Even the election scheduled for this year was canceled when the rubber-stamp National Assembly altered the Constitution to give itself another year of tenure.

In some areas the signs of disaffection are clear enough. Observers of sweeps by the Vietnamese army through the Mekong Delta provinces are often struck by the phenomenon of deserted villages. As troops approach, all flee, except a few old men and children. No one offers information; no one hurries to put out flags. Most of the rural area is controlled by Vietcong, whose agents will move back as soon as the troops have departed.

President Ngo Dinh Diem is well aware of the importance of securing the countryside. His brother has the vision of concentrating peasants into "strategic hamlets" ringed with mud walls, moats and barbed wire. The object is to isolate peasants from the Communists. Brother Ngo Dinh Nhu urged the creation of 8,000 hamlets by the end of this year.

But the American aid mission has advised the regime to come up with a less-expensive plan. While appalled by the dreary regimentation of life in these fortified villages, most Americans are convinced that the strategic hamlet is part of the answer to the pacification problem. They hope to persuade the President that forced labor on hamlet defenses is not the way to win the affection of the peasants.

Besides urging the Government to pay for this labor— workers are not even fed but must provide their own food—the American mission is trying to channel aid directly to the villages in support of counter-insurgency . . .

On the political front Americans are less inventive. Washington insists there is no alternative to President Ngo

Dinh Diem. United States official policy is tied to the status quo. This policy is doomed in the long run, some feel, because the Vietnamese President cannot give his country the inspired leadership needed to defeat the Vietcong.

In the last seven years, the United States has spent well over $2,000,000,000 to prevent a Communist take-over in South Vietnam. Holding the line in Southeast Asia was a major premise of the strategy for containing Communism formulated by John Foster Dulles, President Eisenhower's Secretary of State, who felt the whole of Southeast Asia would go down the drain unless South Vietnam were saved.

The United States has been deeply involved in South Vietnam ever since 1954 when, after the defeat of the French in the Indochina War, Vietnam was partitioned. The Communists took over North Vietnam. With American support, Ngo Dinh Diem, a strongly anti-Communist aristocrat, rose to power in the South.

Few Americans in Saigon during the first chaotic years of President Ngo Dinh Diem's leadership had much confidence in his ability to survive. In 1955, President Eisenhower's special representative in South Vietnam, Gen. J. Lawton Collins, recommended that the United States withhold support from the aloof and obstinate Vietnamese leader.

But General Collins' recommendation was countered by reports sent to Allen W. Dulles, then director of the Central Intelligence Agency, by Col. (now Brig. Gen.) Edward G. Lansdale, the chief United States intelligence agent in Saigon. Colonel Lansdale saw no alternative to Ngo Dinh Diem. Allen Dulles persuaded his brother, the Secretary of State, that Colonel Lansdale was right and General Collins was wrong.

Those who recall conditions in Saigon at the time may now agree that Colonel Lansdale was right. Ngo Dinh Diem's rivals were either notoriously corrupt, or tagged as collaborators in the former French colonial regime, or lacking in popular appeal. Ngo Dinh Diem had some following among the Catholic refugees from North Vietnam, and these were at least reliably anti-Communist.

The little President has shown a remarkable talent for surviving coups and assassination attempts. He got rid of Emperor Bao Dai, established control over the army, won a small war against gangster elements of the Saigon police, eliminated the private armies of two powerful religious sects, the Cao Dai and Hoa Hao, and resettled a million refugees from the north.

In the relatively quiet years between 1955 and 1958, when the Communist insurrection supported by North Vietnam began, South Vietnam made some modest economic progress. Saigon looked relatively prosperous. But United States economic aid was slow to reach the villages. And Ngo Dinh Diem did little to generate enthusiasm for his regime.

By last year the Communists controlled most of the countryside. The Vietnamese President was forced to ask for greatly increased military aid. President Kennedy responded by rushing thousands of United States military personnel to South Vietnam to serve as advisers and instructors. A United States Military Assistance Command was established under Gen. Paul Donal Harkins.

Should the situation disintegrate further, Washington may face the alternative of ditching Ngo Dinh Diem for a military junta or sending combat troops to bolster the regime.

No one who has seen conditions of combat in South Vietnam would expect conventionally trained United States forces to fight any better against Communist guerrillas than did the French in their seven years of costly and futile warfare. For, despite all the talk here of training men for jungle fighting, of creating counter-guerrillas, who can exist in forests and swamps and hunt down the Vietcong, Americans may simply lack the endurance and the motivation to meet the unbelievably tough demands of jungle fighting.

The Tonkin Gulf Incident Address
By President Lyndon B. Johnson
August 8, 1964

On August 2, 1964, the American destroyer the Maddox *was conducting an espionage mission in the waters of the Gulf of Tonkin, a key body of water lying off the east coast of North Vietnam. Initial readings from equipment aboard the* Maddox *reported that the ship had been fired upon, most likely from North Vietnamese patrol boats in the area. The* Maddox *and another U.S. destroyer, the C. Turner Joy, began firing into the night rapidly, with American warplanes from the USS* Ticonderoga *supporting the showcase of American firepower. However, hours later, the captain of the* Maddox *concluded that there might not have been an actual attack.*

Following the incident, President Lyndon Johnson went to Congress to ask for official orders to move into Vietnam. Johnson pleaded with Congress, addressing the attack on the Maddox *as pure aggression by the North Vietnamese. On August 7, the Tonkin Gulf Resolution passed, 416 to 0 by the House and 88 to 2 by the Senate. The resolution stipulated that the president of the United States could "take all necessary measures to repel armed attack against the forces of the United States and to prevent further aggression."*

The Tonkin Gulf Resolution opened the door for full escalation of U.S. involvement in Vietnam. Immediately after the resolution was passed, the United States would be fully committed to a war in Vietnam. By July 1965, 80,000 American troops would be mobilized and operating in South Vietnam. The following is a copy of President Johnson's address to Congress on the Tonkin Gulf incident.

———◻———

Last night I announced to the American people that the North Vietnamese regime had conducted further deliberate attacks against U.S. naval vessels operating in international waters, and I had therefore directed air action against gunboats and supporting facilities used in these hostile operations. This air action has now been carried out with substantial damage to the boats and facilities. Two U.S. aircraft were lost in the action.

After consultation with the leaders of both parties in the Congress, I further announced a decision to ask the Congress for a resolution expressing the unity and determination of the United States in supporting freedom and in protecting peace in southeast Asia.

These latest actions of the North Vietnamese regime have given a new and grave turn to the already serious situation in southeast Asia. Our commitments in that area are well known to the Congress. They were first made in 1954 by President Eisenhower. They were further defined in the Southeast Asia Collective Defense Treaty approved by the Senate in February 1955.

This treaty with its accompanying protocol obligates the United States and other members to act in accordance with their constitutional processes to meet Communist aggression against any of the parties or protocol states.

Our policy in southeast Asia has been consistent and unchanged since 1955. I summarized it on June 2 in four simple propositions:

1. America keeps her word. Here as elsewhere, we must and shall honor our commitments.

2. The issue is the future of southeast Asia as a whole. A threat to any nation in that region is a threat to all and a threat to us.

3. Our purpose is peace. We have no military, political, or territorial ambitions in the area.

4. This is not just a jungle war, but a struggle for freedom on every front of human activity. Our military and economic assistance to South Vietnam and Laos in particular has the purpose of helping these countries to repel aggression and strengthen their independence.

The threat to the free nations of southeast Asia has long been clear. The North Vietnamese regime has constantly sought to take over South Vietnam and Laos. This Communist regime has violated the Geneva accords for Vietnam. It has systematically conducted a campaign of subversion, which includes the direction, training, and supply of personnel and arms for the conduct of guerrilla warfare in South Vietnamese territory. In Laos, the North Vietnamese regime has maintained military forces, used Laotian territory for infiltration into South Vietnam, and most recently carried out combat operations—all in direct violation of the Geneva Agreements of 1962.

In recent months, the actions of the North Vietnamese regime have become steadily more threatening . . .

As President of the United States I have concluded that I should now ask the Congress, on its part, to join in affirming the national determination that all such attacks will be met, and that the United States will continue in its basic policy of assisting the free nations of the area to defend their freedom.

As I have repeatedly made clear, the United States intends no rashness, and seeks no wider war. We must make it clear to all that the United States is united in its determination to bring about the end of Communist subversion and aggression in the area. We seek the full and effective restoration of the international agreements signed in Geneva in 1954, with respect to South Vietnam, and again in Geneva in 1962, with respect to Laos . . .

"The Secret Side of the Tonkin Gulf Incident"
By Dale Andrade and Kenneth Conboy
From Naval History, *August 1999*

What the public knew about the Tonkin Gulf incident and, more important, what Congress knew about the incident was in sharp contrast to the reality of the situation. Authors Dale Andrade, a Vietnam War historian, and Kenneth Conboy, a former analyst with the Washington-based Asian Studies Center, attempted to uncover President Johnson's justifications for massive troop deployment to Vietnam. According to the authors, there were many Desoto missions taking place in the Tonkin waters at the time. ("Desoto" was the code name for secret reconnaissance missions such as the one the Maddox was on.) These missions had begun under the Central Intelligence Agency in 1961 but were not specifically made known to Congress. The Desoto missions were used not only to gather intelligence but also to sabotage (and eavesdrop on) North Vietnam's shore-based communications. The following excerpt details a few such missions, including the Tonkin Gulf incident, in which the United States was not the innocent bystander that President Johnson made it out to be in his address to Congress.

In July 1964, Operational Plan 34A was taking off, but during the first six months of this highly classified program of covert attacks against North Vietnam, one after the other, missions failed, often spelling doom for the commando teams inserted into the North by boat and parachute.

These secret intelligence-gathering missions and sabotage operations had begun under the Central Intelligence Agency (CIA) in 1961, but in January 1964, the program was transferred to the Defense Department under the control of a covert organization called the Studies and Observations Group (SOG). For the maritime part of the covert operation, nasty-class fast patrol boats were purchased quietly from Norway to lend the illusion that the United States was not involved in the operations.

To increase the chances of success, SOG proposed increased raids along the coast, emphasizing offshore bombardment by the boats rather than inserting commandos. In Saigon, General William C. Westmoreland, the new commander of Military Assistance Command, Vietnam (MACV), approved of the plan, and SOG began testing 81-mm mortars, 4.5-inch rockets, and recoilless rifles aboard the boats.

Under cover of darkness, four boats (PTF-2, PTF-3, PTF-5, and PTF-6) left Da Nang, racing north up the coast toward the demilitarized zone (DMZ), then angling farther out to sea as they left the safety of South Vietnamese waters. About five hours later they neared their objective: the offshore islands of Hon Me and Hon Nieu.

Just before midnight, the four boats cut their engines. To the northwest, though they could not see it in the blackness, was Hon Me; to the southwest lay Hon Nieu. The crews quietly made last-minute plans, then split up. It was 20 minutes into the new day, 31 July, when PTF-3 and PTF-6, both under the command of Lieutenant Son—considered one of the best boat skippers in the covert fleet—reached Hon Me and began their run at the shore. Even in the darkness, the commandos could see their target—a water tower surrounded by a few military buildings.

Suddenly, North Vietnamese guns opened fire from the shore. Heavy machine-gun bullets riddled PTF-6, tearing away part of the port bow and wounding four South Vietnamese crewmen, including Lieutenant Son. Moments later, one of the crewmen spotted a North Vietnamese Swatow patrol boat bearing down on them. There was no way to get a commando team ashore to plant demolition charges; they would have to do what damage they could with the boats' guns.

Illumination rounds shot skyward, catching the patrol boats in their harsh glare. But the light helped the commandos as well, revealing their targets. Holding their vector despite the gunfire, the boats rushed in, pouring 20-mm and 40-mm fire and 57-mm recoilless rifle rounds into their target. In less than 25 minutes, the attack was over. PTF-3 and PTF-6 broke off and streaked south for safety; they were back in port before 1200.

At Hon Nieu, the attack was a complete surprise. Just after midnight on 31 July, PTF-2 and PTF-5, commanded by Lieutenant Huyet, arrived undetected at a position 800 yards northeast of the island. Moving in closer, the crew could see their target—a communications tower—silhouetted in the moonlight. Both boats opened fire, scoring hits on the tower, then moved on to other buildings nearby. The only opposition came from a few scattered machine guns on shore, but they did no damage. Forty-five minutes after beginning their attack, the commandos withdrew. The two boats headed northeast along the same route they had come, then turned south for the run back to South Vietnam.

North Vietnam Reacts

Within days, Hanoi lodged a complaint with the International Control Commission (ICC), which had been established in 1954 to oversee the provisions of the Geneva Accords. The United States denied involvement.

In response, the North Vietnamese built up their naval presence around the offshore islands. On 3 August, the CIA confirmed that "Hanoi's naval units have displayed increasing sensitivity to U.S. and South Vietnamese naval activity in the Gulf of Tonkin during the past several months."

At about the same time, there were other "secret" missions going on. Codenamed Desoto, they were special U.S. Navy patrols designed to eavesdrop on enemy shore-based communications—specifically China, North Korea, and now North Vietnam. Typically, the missions were carried out by a destroyer specially outfitted with sensitive eavesdropping equipment.

The Maddox Heads North

On 28 July, the latest specially fitted destroyer, the *Maddox* (DD-731), set out from Taiwan for the South China Sea. Three days later, she rendezvoused with a tanker just east of the DMZ before beginning her intelligence-gathering mission up the North Vietnamese coast. The *Maddox* planned to sail to 16 points along the North Vietnam coast, ranging from the DMZ north to the Chinese border. At each point, the ship would stop and circle, picking up electronic signals before moving on. Everything went smoothly until the early hours of 2 August, when intelligence picked up indications that the North Vietnamese Navy had moved additional Swatows into the vicinity of Hon Me and Hon Nieu Islands and ordered them to prepare for battle. This was almost certainly a reaction to the recent 34A raids.

At 0354 on 2 August, the destroyer was just south of Hon Me Island. Captain John J. Herrick, Commander Destroyer Division 192, embarked in the *Maddox*, concluded that there would be "possible hostile action." He headed seaward hoping to avoid a confrontation until daybreak, then returned to the coast at 1045, this time north of Hon Me. It is difficult to imagine that the North Vietnamese could come to any other conclusion than that the 34A and Desoto missions were all part of the same operation.

The *Maddox* was attacked at 1600. Ship's radar detected five patrol boats, which turned out to be P-4 torpedo boats and Swatows. When the enemy boats closed to less than 10,000 yards, the destroyer fired three shots across the bow of the lead vessel. In response, the North Vietnamese boat launched a torpedo. The *Maddox* fired again—this time to kill—hitting the second North Vietnamese boat just as it launched two torpedoes. Badly damaged, the boat limped home. Changing course in time to evade the torpedoes, the *Maddox* again was attacked, this time by a boat that fired another torpedo and 14.5-mm machine guns. The bullets struck the destroyer; the torpedo missed. As the enemy boat passed astern, it was raked by gunfire from the *Maddox* that killed the boat's commander.

The battle was over in 22 minutes. The North Vietnamese turned for shore with the *Maddox* in pursuit. Aircraft from the *Ticonderoga* (CVA-14) appeared on the scene, strafing three torpedo boats and sinking the one that had been damaged in the battle with the *Maddox*.

Making the Connection

North Vietnam immediately and publicly linked the 34A raids and the Desoto patrol, a move that threatened tentative peace feelers from Washington that were only just reaching Hanoi. The Johnson administration had made the first of several secret diplomatic attempts during the summer of 1964 to convince the North Vietnamese to stop its war on South Vietnam, using the chief Canadian delegate to the ICC, J. Blair Seaborn, to pass the message along to Hanoi. After the Tonkin Gulf incident, the State Department cabled Seaborn, instructing him to tell the North Vietnamese that "neither the *Maddox* or any other destroyer was in any way associated with any attack on the DRV [Democratic Republic of Vietnam, or North Vietnam] islands." This was the first of several carefully worded official statements aimed at separating 34A and Desoto and leaving the impression that the United States was not involved in the covert operations.

The U.S. Navy stressed that the two technically were not in communication with one another, but the distinction was irrelevant to the North Vietnamese. Both were perceived as threats, and both were in the same general area at about the same time.

CIA Director John McCone was convinced that Hanoi was reacting to the raids when it attacked the *Maddox*. During a meeting at the White House on the evening of 4 August, President Johnson asked McCone, "Do they want a war by attacking our ships in the middle of the Gulf of Tonkin?"

"No," replied McCone. "The North Vietnamese are reacting defensively to our attacks on their offshore islands . . . The attack is a signal to us that the North Vietnamese have the will and determination to continue the war." It took only a little imagination to see why the North Vietnamese might connect the two. In this case, perception was much more important than reality.

The North Vietnamese Ministry of Foreign Affairs made all this clear in September when it published a "Memorandum Regarding the U.S. War Acts Against the Democratic Republic of Vietnam in the First Days of August 1964." Hanoi pointed out what Washington denied: "On July 30, 1964 . . . U.S. and South Vietnamese warships intruded into the territorial waters of the Democratic Republic of Vietnam and simultaneously shelled: Hon Nieu Island, 4 kilometers off the coast of Thanh Hoa Province [and] Hon Me Island, 12 kilometers off the coast of Thanh Hoa Province." It also outlined the *Maddox*'s path along the coast on 2 August and the 34A attacks on Vinh Son the following day. Hanoi denied the charge that it had fired on the U.S. destroyers on 4 August, calling the charge "an impudent fabrication."

At the White House, administration officials panicked as the public spotlight illuminated their policy in Vietnam and threatened to reveal its covert roots. President Johnson ordered a halt to all 34A operations "to avoid sending confusing signals associated with recent events in the Gulf of Tonkin." If there had been any doubt before about whose hand was behind the raids, surely there was none now.

Congress Reacts

Of course, none of this was known to Congress, which demanded an explanation for the goings-on in the Tonkin Gulf. On 6 August, Secretary of Defense Robert S. McNamara told a joint session of the Senate Foreign Relations and Armed Services Committees that the North Vietnamese attack on the *Maddox* was " . . . no isolated event. They are part and parcel of a continuing Communist drive to conquer South Vietnam . . ." McNamara did not mention the 34A raids.

The fig leaf of plausible denial served McNamara in this case, but it was scant cover. Hanoi was more than willing to tell the world about the attacks, and it took either a fool or an innocent to believe that the United States knew nothing about the raids. Despite McNamara's nimble answers, North Vietnam's insistence that there was a connection between 34A and the Desoto patrols was only natural.

Despite [Senator Wayne] Morse's doubts, Senate reaction fell in behind the Johnson team, and the question of secret operations was overtaken by the issue of punishing Hanoi for its blatant attack on a U.S. warship in international waters. On 7 August, the Senate passed the Tonkin Gulf Resolution, allowing the administration greater latitude in expanding the war by a vote of 88 to 2. Senator Morse was one of the dissenters. The House passed the resolution unanimously.

America's Vietnam War had begun in earnest. Within the year, U.S. bombers would strike North Vietnam, and U.S. ground units would land on South Vietnamese soil. But for a band of South Vietnamese commandos and a handful of U.S. advisers, not much had changed. The publicity caused by the Tonkin Gulf incident and the subsequent resolution shifted attention away from covert activities and ended high-level debate over the wisdom of secret operations against North Vietnam. In the future, conventional operations would receive all the attention. This was the only time covert operations against the North came close to being discussed in public. For the rest of the war they would be truly secret—and in the end they were a dismal failure.

"Aggression from the North"
The U.S. State Department White Paper on Vietnam February 27, 1965

Issued by the U.S. State Department on February 27, 1965, this "white paper" (government document) attempts to officially explain why the United States was involved in Vietnam.

According to the document, the United States was fighting for freedom in South Vietnam and helping friends that it would not abandon. There was no greater terror during the Cold War than Communism, and the United States, just as it had tried in Korea, found that it had to get involved militarily in order to protect democracy. The report made a point to establish that the South Vietnamese government had been fighting for its survival for ten long years against the North Vietnamese and that it had requested U.S. assistance. The United States wanted initially to be seen as a country that was helping an ally during a time of need, while sending a message to the encroaching specter of Communism. Less than a week after this white paper was issued, Operation Rolling Thunder would unleash a massive U.S. bombing campaign in North Vietnam.

———□———

South Vietnam is fighting for its life against a brutal campaign of terror and armed attack inspired, directed, supplied, and controlled by the Communist regime in Hanoi. This flagrant aggression has been going on for years, but recently the pace has quickened and the threat has now become acute.

The war in Vietnam is a new kind of war, a fact as yet poorly understood in most parts of the world. Much of the confusion that prevails in the thinking of many people, and even governments, stems from this basic misunderstanding. For in Vietnam a totally new brand of aggression has been loosed against an independent people who want to make their way in peace and freedom.

Vietnam is not another Greece, where indigenous guerrilla forces used friendly neighboring territory as a sanctuary.

Vietnam is not another Malaya, where Communist guerrillas were, for the most part, physically distinguishable from the peaceful majority they sought to control.

Vietnam is not another Philippines, where Communist guerrillas were physically separated from the source of their moral and physical support.

Above all, the war in Vietnam is not a spontaneous and local rebellion against the established government.

There are elements in the Communist program of conquest directed against South Vietnam common to each of the previous areas of aggression and subversion. But there is one fundamental difference. In Vietnam a Communist government has set out deliberately to conquer a sovereign people in a neighboring state. And to achieve its end, it has used every resource of its own government to carry out its carefully planned program of concealed aggression. North Vietnam's commitment to seize control of the South is no less total than was the commitment of the regime in North Korea in 1950. But knowing the consequences of the latter's undisguised attack, the planners in Hanoi have tried desperately to conceal their hand. They have failed and their aggression is as real as that of an invading army.

This report is a summary of the massive evidence of North Vietnamese aggression obtained by the Government of South Vietnam. This evidence has been jointly analyzed by South Vietnamese and American experts.

The evidence shows that the hard core of the Communist forces attacking South Vietnam were trained in the North and ordered into the South by Hanoi. It shows that the key leadership of the Vietcong (VC), the officers and much of the cadre, many of the technicians, political

organizers, and propagandists have come from the North
and operate under Hanoi's direction. It shows that the training
of essential military personnel and their infiltration into the
South is directed by the Military High Command in Hanoi.
In recent months new types of weapons have been introduced
in the VC army, for which all ammunition must come from
outside sources. Communist China and other Communist
states have been the prime suppliers of these weapons and
ammunition, and they have been channeled primarily
through North Vietnam.

The directing force behind the effort to conquer South
Vietnam is the Communist Party in the North, the Lao Dong
(Workers) Party. As in every Communist state, the party is an
integral part of the regime itself. North Vietnamese officials
have expressed their firm determination to absorb South
Vietnam into the Communist world.

Through its Central Committee, which controls the
Government of the North, the Lao Dong Party directs the
total political and military effort of the Vietcong. The Military
High Command in the North trains the military men and
sends them into South Vietnam. The Central Research
Agency, North Vietnam's central intelligence organization,
directs the elaborate espionage and subversion effort . . .

Under Hanoi's overall direction the Communists have
established an extensive machine for carrying on the war
within South Vietnam. The focal point is the Central Office for
South Vietnam with its political and military subsections and
other specialized agencies. A subordinate part of this Central

Office is the Liberation Front for South Vietnam. The front was formed at Hanoi's order in 1960. Its principle function is to influence opinion abroad and to create the false impression that the aggression in South Vietnam is an indigenous rebellion against the established Government.

For more than 10 years the people and the Government of South Vietnam, exercising the inherent right of self-defense, have fought back against these efforts to extend Communist power south across the 17th parallel. The United States has responded to the appeals of the Government of the Republic of Vietnam for help in this defense of the freedom and independence of its land and its people.

In 1961 the Department of State issued a report called "A Threat to the Peace." It described North Vietnam's program to seize South Vietnam. The evidence in that report had been presented by the Government of the Republic of Vietnam to the International Control Commission (ICC). A special report by the ICC in June 1962 upheld the validity of that evidence. The Commission held that there was "sufficient evidence to show beyond reasonable doubt" that North Vietnam had sent arms and men into South Vietnam to carry out subversion with the aim of overthrowing the legal Government there. The ICC found the authorities in Hanoi in specific violation of four provisions of the Geneva Accords of 1954.

Since then, new and even more impressive evidence of Hanoi's aggression has accumulated. The Government of the United States believes that evidence should be presented to its own citizens and to the world. It is important for free men to know what has been happening in Vietnam, and how, and why. That is the purpose of this report . . .

The record is conclusive. It establishes beyond question that North Vietnam is carrying out a carefully conceived plan of aggression against the South. It shows that North Vietnam has intensified its efforts in the years since it was condemned by the International Control Commission. It proves that Hanoi continues to press its systematic program of armed aggression into South Vietnam. This aggression violates the United Nations Charter. It is directly contrary to the Geneva Accords of 1954 and of 1962 to which North Vietnam is a party. It is a fundamental threat to the freedom and security of South Vietnam.

The people of South Vietnam have chosen to resist this threat. At their request, the United States has taken its place beside them in their defensive struggle.

The United States seeks no territory, no military bases, no favored position. But we have learned the meaning of aggression elsewhere in the post-war world, and we have met it.

If peace can be restored in South Vietnam, the United States will be ready at once to reduce its military involvement. But it will not abandon friends who want to remain free. It will do what must be done to help them. The choice now between peace and continued and increasingly destructive conflict is one for the authorities in Hanoi to make.

CHAPTER TWO

INDIVIDUALS, GROUPS, AND INSTITUTIONS: THE WAR IN THE JUNGLE, 1965–1968

"An Endless, Relentless War"
From The Making of a Quagmire: America and Vietnam During the Kennedy Era
By David Halberstam
1987

The following piece introduces us to the reality of war in the Vietnam jungle against the Vietcong, the guerrilla Communist forces of North Vietnam. Excerpted from his acclaimed book The Making of a Quagmire, *Pulitzer Prize–winning journalist David Halberstam observes that South Vietnam (with the United States at its side) had the hardware and the technological advantage over the Vietcong. But the Vietcong had something that was even more important: support of Vietnam's enormous peasant population. Using propaganda as a weapon, the Vietcong built an army of peasants and armed them with fear and hatred of the occupying American forces. Even as the reporter spends the day in what he thinks is a "successful" mission, others in his group are less impressed because victories are not always what they seem.*

Whereas a normal military campaign is decided by which side suffers the most casualties, the combat war in Vietnam was vastly different. The line between victory and defeat was blurred in the jungles of Vietnam.

The first time you met a member of the Vietcong there was a sharp sense of disappointment. He was not, it turned out, very different; he was simply another Vietnamese. When you saw him he was usually either kneeling and firing at you, or he had just been captured—or, more often than not, he was dead: the bodies were always lined up, their feet in an orderly row. The guerrilla wore little, perhaps a simple peasant Dajaina suit, perhaps only shorts. He was slim and wiry, and his face would remind you of your interpreter or of that taxi driver who drove you to My Tho. Only the haircut was different, very thin along the sides, and very long on top and in front. It was a bad haircut, and like the frailness of the uniform and the thin wallet with perhaps only a few pictures of some peasant woman, it made the enemy human. But one's sympathy did not last long; this was the same face that had been seen by the outnumbered defenders of some small outpost before it was overrun.

There were not many operations in which the Vietcong were caught; few prisoners were taken in this war. One of the few exceptions to this that I ever observed took place in April 1963, when I accompanied the new armed-helicopter units in the upper Camau peninsula on what were known as Eagle flights. An Eagle flight was risky business; it meant that a small number of elite troops circled above the paddies in the choppers, looking for likely targets. When an objective was sighted the helicopters dropped out of the sky, virtually on top of a hamlet, and the troops made a quick search, probing and outing. If the enemy was there, other regular units, waiting in the rear with other helicopters, would be thrown in quickly. But dropping swiftly out of the sky and exploring the unknown with a handful of troops was sometimes terrifying; the helicopters have the visibility of a press box, but you were watching a war instead of a football game. When you plunged earthward, little men sometimes rushed to different positions, kneeled and started firing at the press box while your own tracers sought them out.

On that day in April the 21st Recon Company, a particularly good outfit composed largely of troops who had fought with the Vietminh during the Indochina war, was with us. We were scouting a Vietcong battalion, moving along a line of villages which we thought the battalion had been using as its main line of communication in that region. But this was the upper Camau, almost completely enemy territory, where one could find a Vietcong squad in virtually every village.

It is perhaps deceptive to use a word like "battalion" here; when such a unit attacked a given point it might number three hundred men, but immediately afterward it would break up into small groups slipping into neighboring villages and awaiting the signal for the next operation. A single large force would make too good a target for the Government; besides, by splitting up, more men could indoctrinate more peasants, and no single village would have to take on the task of feeding three hundred extra mouths . . .

The next two villages produced only some crude grenades made by an old farmer. "The local guerrilla," said the Vietnamese captain. These were the lowest of the three types of Vietcong: they farmed in the day and fought at night, and they had the worst weapons. When I first came to Vietnam their arms were all homemade; by the time I left they were using French equipment and even some American M-I's. But even in April 1963, in a village where there were no other weapons, a homemade grenade or a rusty rifle had great power.

The local guerrillas were a vital part of the Vietcong apparatus. They gave the village a sense of Communist continuity, they could provide intelligence on Government activities and serve as a local security force for a traveling commissar, or they could guide the professional Vietcong troops. This last was particularly important to the success and mobility of the guerrillas; everywhere they went they had trained, local guides to steer them through seemingly impenetrable areas. Because of these local men the enemy's troops could often move twenty-five miles in five hours—which meant that a raiding force attacking at night was almost impossible to find by daylight. These local guerrillas were also part of the propaganda network, for in a village they might be the only ones with a radio. (Sometimes it was only the shell of a radio, but the local man would pretend he could hear news and would give out information of Vietcong victories.)

We flew back to the base to refuel, and then returned to the area. Shortly before noon we hit pay dirt. Out of one village came a flock of Vietcong, running across the paddies, and there was intense fire from the treeline. While five of our ships emptied their troops, the rest of the choppers strafed the area. Soon the guerrillas broke from their positions and ran for a nearby canal, where they might find hiding places. We came hurtling down on them at a hundred miles an hour, just a few feet off the ground. We were still drawing fire, but it was more sporadic now.

We bore down on one fleeing Vietcong. The paddy's surface was rough and his run was staggered, like that of a good but drunken broken-field runner against imaginary tacklers. We came closer and closer; inside the helicopter I could almost hear him gasping for breath, and as we bore down I could see the heaving of his body. It was like watching a film of one of your own nightmares, but in this case we were the pursuers rather than the pursued. The copilot fired his machine guns but missed, and the man kept going. Then there was a flash of orange and a blast of heat inside the ship, and the helicopter heaved from the recoil of its rockets. When they exploded the man fell. He lay still as we went over him, but when we turned he scrambled to his feet, still making for the canal, now only about fifty yards away. While we circled and swept toward him again he was straining for the bank, like a runner nearing the finish line. We had one last shot at him. Our copilot fired one last burst of the machine gun as the guerrilla made a desperate surge. The bullets cut him down as he reached the canal, and his body skidded on the hard bank as he collapsed.

We turned and circled again. All over the paddies helicopters were rounding up Vietcong soldiers. We landed near the village which other members of the Recon company were searching. The troops were gentler with the population than most ARVN (Army of the Republic of Vietnam—the South Vietnamese) soldiers I had seen; in front of one hut a medic was giving aid to a wounded guerrilla.

"I have never taken this many prisoners before," the Vietnamese captain said. There were sixteen of them. He turned to one of his men. "Show the American the poor little farmer," he said. They brought in a wiry young man. "This one says he is a farmer," the officer said. He pushed the young man in front of me and flipped the prisoner's palms over. "He has very soft hands for a farmer," the captain said. "He has the hands of a bar girl in Saigon. He is not a very good soldier yet. In a few months, though, he might have been very good."

The prisoner was beginning to tremble. The conversation in a foreign language obviously frightened him, and I was sure that this was why the captain was using English. I asked the captain what kind of enemy we had surprised. "Territorial," he said. This was the middle rank of Vietcong guerrillas; we called them provincial guerrillas. They operated in groups of up to one hundred and were often attached to the hard-core units to beef up their strength for a major attack; they would also hit smaller outposts.

"The leadership was not very good," the captain said. "If it had been a hard-core unit, there would have been more fighting and more dying. I think we surprised them."

Before we took off again, I walked over to the canal. The little soldier's body had actually crossed the finish line; his shoulder was over the bank, his blood was still running into the canal and there was a look of agony on his face . . .

"Infiltration: The Long Journey South" From North Vietnam's Strategy for Survival
By Jon M. Van Dyke
1972

Without adequate air support and transportation, the North Vietnamese had to infiltrate South Vietnam in a manner that was not only time-consuming and arduous but extremely dangerous for those involved. As the United States ran air strikes and decimated the North's supply, energy, and troop locations, the Vietcong made a concentrated effort to make their way into the South. At first, there was only minimal infiltration of North Vietnamese troops into South Vietnam. But in 1965, the North felt that the effort had to be made to increase its troop and supply movement south if it wanted to sway the war in its favor. This excerpt details how the Vietcong survived not only American air strikes but also the harsh Vietnam jungle and elements. They made their way south through many avenues, but the most famous was the so-called Ho Chi Minh Trail, which cut into the neighboring country of Laos. This Vietcong

*transport route, which snaked through thousands of miles of
dense jungle, somehow endured the massive American bombing
campaign. The war would only grow as North Vietnamese
troops and armaments continued to reach southern forces
through this vital supply line.*

———□———

Infiltration of North Vietnamese to the South did not begin until
the escalation of the war in early 1965. Prior to that time, about
40,000 of the South Vietnamese who had gone to North Vietnam
after the 1954 division of Vietnam (who are referred to in negoti-
ating jargon as "regroupees") had worked their way back to the
South to serve as cadre for the Viet Cong, and supplies were
moving regularly from North to South Vietnam. Virtually no
members of the North Vietnamese regular army had, however,
made the trip.

The infiltration situation changed in 1965, partly because
the North Vietnamese thought that year would be decisive and
partly because large numbers of American troops arrived in
South Vietnam to thwart a Communist victory. From a previous
annual high of 12,900, the infiltration rose (according to U.S.
estimates) to 35,300 during 1965, to 89,000 in 1966, to
between 59,000 and 90,000 in 1967, and then to about 150,000
in 1968. In June 1966, Secretary McNamara announced that the
number of trucks moving from North to South Vietnam was
twice as large as it had been when the bombing started . . .

The rapid build-up of forces in the first half of 1968
changed the situation somewhat; the new troops could not get
all their supplies from the traditional sources and were forced to
rely more on the routes from the North. There were shortages of

guns and ammunition among the Communist forces in South Vietnam just before the summer of 1968, and occasional reports of food shortages. Vast new road complexes were quickly opened in the Communist-held areas, however, and at any given moment during the first half of 1968, 10,000 trucks were carrying supplies south through Laos and South Vietnam. An American Army captain who was fighting in the Saigon area in September 1968 said of the Communist supply situation: "Those newer weapons they have are damned good. And don't believe anyone who tells you that they have an ammunition or food problem. They don't." Even after the build-up, the North Vietnamese had to send no more than 80 tons of supplies from the North to sustain their troops.

Before going south, each North Vietnamese soldier is given particularly nourishing food for a period of two weeks to two months to strengthen him for the arduous journey. One private who left for the South in August 1965 said that his food allowance was quadrupled for two months so that he could eat anything he wanted, including beef, pork, fish, cake, fruits, sweets, sugar, and milk. Sometimes a soldier about to go south is granted permission to visit his family for a few days before the trip begins, but more often there is no opportunity to say good-by. When a trip home is permitted, the soldier is frequently instructed not to tell his family that he is going south. The dependent families of soldiers fighting in South Vietnam receive some support from the central government—at least for a while—but almost no mail gets back to North Vietnam from the soldiers fighting in the South, and only a few of the soldiers who go south ever come back.

In a typical trip south, a soldier travels by train or truck from his training camp to Dong Hoi, the southernmost city of any size in North Vietnam. Then he begins walking south and southwest on paved and unpaved roads—traveling only at night because of the danger of air attacks—to a settlement at the northwest corner of the demilitarized zone. At this settlement, which the American intelligence community calls "Ho Village," he will rest for a few days, receive new clothing and equipment, and identification documents to camouflage his identity as a North Vietnamese. After this rest, the infiltrator crosses into Laos, where he and his companions are guided through the hundreds of small paths and roads in the complex known as the Ho Chi Minh Trail. Here the infiltrators can travel by day because of the thick jungle canopy which covers the area, and at night they stay at campsites which are situated along the paths at 10- to 15-mile intervals. These way stations consist of two or three huts guarded by a small squadron of soldiers. Every few stations has a storehouse full of rice to supply the infiltrators as they pass.

On a typical day during the march through Laos, the soldiers rise at 3:30 in the morning, march from 4 to 11, and then, after a lunch break, continue marching until 6 in the evening. At that time, they put up hammocks, dig foxholes, cook and eat dinner, prepare their rice-ball lunches for the following day, and then sleep. The marchers cover 10 to 15 miles per day and rest one day out of every five to ten. Their food, both during the march, and after reaching the South, consists of one to two pounds of rice per day, plus some vegetables, salt, and meat.

The infiltrators face some problems common to any long march. Provided with sandals rather than boots, they are subject to blisters and sprained ankles until they learn how to use the sandals. They carry some dry field rations, like canned meat and salt, and usually eat two hot and one pre-cooked meal per day. There are frequent shortages, however, and to maintain this diet the soldiers must on occasion obtain rice from the surrounding area, pick wild vegetables, and hunt animals. One infiltrator who subsequently defected reported that his group hunted deer and threw grenades into rivers to catch fish. Health is also a constant problem. Soldiers are reminded at every turn to boil their water, take their anti-malaria pills, and follow anti-mosquito instructions.

Other problems are unique to this particular march. The infiltrators must carry from 75 to 85 pounds of supplies throughout the trip. Among the personal supplies each soldier brings with him are three shirts, three pairs of trousers, a hammock, a pair of sandals, perhaps a nylon tent and a rain-coat, and a first-aid kit filled with various pills. In addition, each soldier must carry a carbine, submachine gun or rifle, and parts of the heavy weapons the company transports south. If one of the marchers becomes too ill to continue, the others must take up his burden. Two soldiers are obliged to carry the sick marcher on a stretcher (while continuing to carry their original load), and the sick soldier's supplies are divided between two other marchers.

Because air attacks on the Ho Chi Minh Trail are a constant threat, troop staging areas must not become congested.

This raises serious logistical problems because, with all the bridges along the Trail under constant aerial attack, the troops are forced to ferry across the many rivers in the area and must assemble at the ferry crossings to wait for the boats. Until October 31, 1968, 150 U.S. planes bombed the Ho Chi Minh Trail in Laos each day; after that date, when the daily bombing of North Vietnam stopped, the U.S. shifted more of its planes to Laos, flying 450 sorties against Laos each day . . .

Interrogation of North Vietnamese prisoners has disclosed that from 10 to 20 per cent of the men sent south do not survive the two- to six-month march to the battle area. Most of those who do not make it succumb to malaria; only 2 per cent are casualties of the air attacks. The cadres leading the troops have tried to brighten the journey by organizing banjo songfests and by providing each squad with a deck of cards. A more significant step to lessen the ordeal of the trip was taken in early 1968 when some infiltrators began riding through Laos by truck rather than marching.

"Death in the Ia Drang Valley"
By Specialist 4/C Jack P. Smith
From the **Saturday Evening Post**
January 28, 1967

In the following piece, Specialist 4/C Jack P. Smith captures a vivid and shockingly detailed firsthand account of a battle in the Ia Drang Valley. It was less of a battle and more of a massacre that wiped out his company between

November 13 and 19, 1965. The idea that war is hell is never more evident than in this dramatic account, which describes how Smith endured both extreme physical and mental suffering as he tried to survive. Many of Smith's fellow soldiers could not endure the anguish, and several took their own lives because of the horror they witnessed. Even Smith admits that there seemed to be no way out of the predicament that these soldiers found themselves in—injured, alone, and surrounded by enemy forces.

———□———

The 1st Battalion had been fighting continuously for three or four days, and I had never seen such filthy troops. Some of them had blood on their faces from scratches and from other guys' wounds. Some had long rips in their clothing where shrapnel and bullets had missed them. They all had that look of shock. They said little, just looked around with darting, nervous eyes.

Whenever I heard a shell coming close, I'd duck, but they'd keep standing. After three days of constant bombardment you get so you can tell from the sound how close a shell is going to land within 50 to 75 feet. There were some wounded lying around, bandaged up with filthy shirts and bandages, smoking cigarettes or lying in a coma with plasma bottles hanging above their stretchers.

The head of the column formed by our battalion was already in the landing zone, which was actually only 30 yards to our left. But our company was still in the woods and elephant grass. I dropped my gear and my ax, which was standard equipment for supply clerks like me. We used them to cut down trees to help make landing zones for our helicopters. The day had grown very hot. I was about one quarter through a smoke when a few shots cracked at the front of the column.

I flipped my cigarette butt, lay down and grabbed my M-16. The fire in front was still growing. Then a few shots were fired right behind me. They seemed to come from the trees. There was firing all over the place now, and I was getting scared. A bullet hit the dirt a foot to my side, and some started whistling over my head.

This wasn't the three or four snipers we had been warned about. There were over 100 North Vietnamese snipers tied in the trees above us—so we learned later—way above us, in the top branches. The firing kept increasing.

Our executive officer (XO) jumped up and said, "Follow me, and let's get the hell out of here." I followed him, along with the rest of the headquarters section and the 1st Platoon. We crouched and ran to the right toward what we thought was the landing zone. But it was only a small clearing—the L.Z. was to our left. We were running deeper into the ambush.

The fire was still increasing. We were all crouched as low as possible, but still keeping up a steady trot, looking from side to side. I glanced back at Richards, one of the company's radio operators. Just as I looked back, he moaned softly and fell to the ground. I knelt down and looked at him, and he shuddered and started to gurgle deep in his stomach. His eyes and tongue popped out, and he died. He had a hole straight through his heart.

I had been screaming for a medic. I stopped. I looked up. Everyone had stopped. All of a sudden all the snipers opened up with automatic weapons. There were PAVN [People's Army of North Vietnam] with machine guns hidden behind every anthill. The noise was deafening.

Then the men started dropping. It was unbelievable. I knelt there staring as at least 20 men dropped within a few seconds. I still had not recovered from the shock of seeing Richards killed, but the jolt of seeing men die so quickly brought me back to life. I hit the dirt fast. The XO was to my left, and Wallace was to my right, with Burroughs to his right. We were touching each other lying there in the tall elephant grass.

Men all around me were screaming. The fire was now a continuous roar. We were even being fired at by our own guys. No one knew where the fire was coming from, and so the men were shooting everywhere. Some were in shock and were blazing away at everything they saw or imagined they saw.

The XO let out a low moan, and his head sank: I felt a flash of panic. I had been assuming that he would get us out of this. Enlisted men may scoff at officers back in the billets, but when the fighting begins, the men automatically become very dependent upon them. Now I felt terribly alone.

The XO had been hit in the small of the back. I ripped off his shirt and there it was: a groove to the right of his spine. The bullet was still in there. He was in a great deal of pain, so a rifleman named Wilson and I removed his gear as best we could, and I bandaged his wound. It was not bleeding much on the outside, but he was very close to passing out.

Just then Wallace let out a "Huh!" A bullet had creased his upper arm and entered his side. He was bleeding in spurts. I ripped away his shirt with my knife and did him up. Then the XO screamed: A bullet had gone through his boot, taking all his toes with it. He was in agony and crying. Wallace was swearing and in shock. I was crying and holding on to the XO's hand to keep from going crazy.

The grass in front of Wallace's head began to fall as if a lawnmower were passing. It was a machine gun, and I could see the vague outline of the Cong's head behind the foot or so of elephant grass. The noise of firing from all directions was so great that I couldn't even hear a machine gun being fired three feet in front of me and one foot above my head.

As if in a dream, I picked up my rifle, put it on automatic, pushed the barrel into the Cong's face and pulled the trigger. I saw his face disappear. I guess I blew his head off but I never saw his body and did not look for it.

Wallace screamed. I had fired the burst pretty close to his ear, but I didn't hit him. Bullets by the thousands were coming from the trees, from the L.Z., from the very ground, it seemed. There was a huge thump nearby. Burroughs rolled over and started a scream, though it sounded more like a growl. He had been lying on his side when a grenade went off about three or four feet from him. He looked as though someone had poured red paint over him from head to toe.

After that everything began getting hazy. I lay there for several minutes, and I think I was beginning to go into shock. I don't remember much.

The amazing thing about all this was that from the time Richards was killed to the time Burroughs was hit, only a minute or two had elapsed. Hundreds of men had been hit all around us, and the sound of men screaming was almost as loud as the firing.

The XO was going fast. He told me his wife's name was Carol. He told me that if he didn't make it, I was to write her and tell her that he loved her. Then he somehow managed to crawl away, saying that he was going to organize the troops. It was his positive decision to do something that reinforced my own will to go on.

Then our artillery and air strikes started to come in. They saved our lives. Just before they started, I could hear North Vietnamese voices on our right. The PAVN battalion was moving in on us, into the woods. The Skyraiders were dropping napalm bombs a hundred feet in front of me on a PAVN machine-gun complex. I felt the hot blast and saw the elephant grass curling ahead of me. The victims were screaming—some of them were our own men who were trapped outside the wood line . . .

"The Tet Offensive"
From The End of the Line: The Siege of Khe Sanh
By Robert Pisor
1982

By 1967, it had become a common practice to declare a truce for a few days during Tet, the Vietnamese New Year, in order to allow the people of both sides to celebrate the holiday with their families. However, in 1968, the North declared a truce but in actuality launched a major offensive during the holiday, which was at the end of January that year. During this offensive, the North attacked every major city in South Vietnam in a highly coordinated effort to turn the tide of the war. The North Vietnamese command envisioned that, after the offensive, civilians in these cities would rise up against the leadership of the South, aiding the North's overthrow of the cities. Luckily for the South, there was no mass civilian uprising against the government, but the Army of South Vietnam (ARVN) did come close to collapse. In the end, the Tet Offensive backfired for the North Vietnamese, who suffered heavy losses.

The Tet Offensive made the brutality of the war very visible to Americans. It also showed that the Communist North was not going to be easily vanquished. Although militarily the Tet Offensive was an American victory, American and South Vietnamese forces suffered heavily. The total number of U.S. casualties in Vietnam during the year 1968 was about 14,000, the highest number for any year of the war. The Tet Offensive was indeed a turning point of the war. But where the war was turning remained unclear. Here, Robert Pisor, an award-winning correspondent for the Detroit News, *captures the chaos as the Tet Offensive exploded across South Vietnam, culminating in the Vietcong's capture of Hue, South Vietnam's most historic city.*

———□———

General Westmoreland was jolted awake at 3 A.M. by the rocket artillery of three enemy divisions in the suburbs of Saigon.

Three thousand Viet Cong soldiers and commando teams were already in the city—striking toward the radio station, the airport, the Presidential Palace, the South Vietnamese military headquarters, the port facilities, and other key targets.

Enemy anti-aircraft guns—big ones, on wheels, with seats for two gunners—jabbed the night sky with green tracers. They had been towed hundreds of miles by hand to be parked at the gates of Tan Son Nhut.

Reports flooded Westmoreland's command center. Hue was under heavy attack—and so were thirty-six of the forty-four provincial capitals in the country. Every major airfield was being hammered by mortars and rockets, and some were fighting off infantry assaults. Soldiers were battling in five of the nation's six autonomous cities, in sixty-four district capitals, and scores of smaller towns. A strong enemy force had hit the Delta city of My Tho, where South Vietnamese President Nguyen Van Thieu was spending the Tet holidays with his family.

The U.S. ambassador had been rushed to a secret hiding place. The U.S. Army's military police, outnumbered and outgunned, were taking heavy casualties in the streets. A Viet Cong sapper team had blasted its way into the U.S. embassy compound, killed four guards, and was now trying to batter down the four-inch-thick teak doors with shoulder-fired rocket grenades.

The shockwaves rippled almost instantly into the Situation Room in the basement of the White House, where President Johnson's assistant for national security affairs, Walt W. Rostow, was giving a late afternoon tour to several *Washington Post* reporters. He had hoped to show them that the war was going much better than the skeptical *Post* was reporting. They were looking at the photomural of Khe Sanh when the first printer chattered out its urgent message. Then another printer spoke, and another. Aides began hurrying in and out. The phone from the Oval Office rang.

The President of the United States wanted to know what the hell was going on . . .

It was now clear to Westmoreland that the enemy's 1967–68 winter-spring campaign would unfold in three separate phases: first, the border battles at Con Thien, Loc Ninh, and Dak To; then a lunatic raid on the cities by the Viet Cong to divert attention; and finally a Dien Bien Phu-style assault by large North Vietnamese forces against Khe Sanh and other I Corps targets. Phase Two was "about to run out of steam," he told news reporters in Saigon on February 1; the enemy had already suffered more than 6,000 casualties.

News that the enemy's hardest blow was yet to come stunned an already sobered Washington. Simultaneous attacks against one hundred cities was an extraordinary military showing for an enemy force that had been described by Westmoreland in recent months as scattered and demoralized. The general had seen "dismay and incredulity" on the faces of reporters in the embassy yard; and now he discovered that the South Vietnamese leadership was paralyzed by the surprise attack. "The government, from President Thieu down through the various ministries, appeared to be stunned."

Westmoreland was becoming more attuned to the magnitude of the Tet Offensive. The enemy seemed willing to spend thousands—maybe even tens of thousands—of soldiers. Heavy fighting was continuing in Saigon, and Hue, and several Delta cities.

Despite Westmoreland's extensive preparations for battle in I Corps in December and January, the situation in the north was worsening.

On January 24, a South Vietnamese military convoy had arrived at Quang Tri City from Saigon—the first through-trip on Route 1 in years. The achievement was announced as an important step in the struggle to secure the roads from Viet Cong interdiction.

At 3 A.M. on January 31, enemy sappers dynamited twenty-five bridges and eleven culverts on Route 1 between Da Nang and Hue. Teams of saboteurs cut an eight-inch pipeline that carried aviation fuel to the thirsty helicopters of the 1st Air Cavalry Division—and torched a tank farm with fifty thousand barrels of fuel.

American forces in the north needed twenty-six hundred tons of supplies every day, not including petroleum, oil, and lubricants, and another one thousand tons a day to prepare for Operation Pegasus—the relief of Khe Sanh. In a single stroke, the daily disgorgement was squeezed off to a trickle.

The logistics situation turned critical almost immediately.

"Achieving a high measure of surprise," three enemy battalions smashed into Quang Tri City, the capital of South Vietnam's northernmost province and a key transshipment point for Marine and Army supplies. ARVN troops blunted the badly coordinated enemy attack, but the fate of the city was still in doubt in the early afternoon. Heavy fog, or the need to guard enormous quantities of newly delivered equipment, kept nearby American units from joining the fight.

The only U.S. forces immediately available were the two 1st Air Cav battalions pushing toward Khe Sanh. They shut down the firebases they had built the day before, turned their backs on the combat base, and flew back to Quang Tri City—air-assaulting into intense enemy fire. They routed the attackers, killing 900 North Vietnamese.

The fighting was worst in Hue.

Eight Viet Cong and North Vietnamese battalions— probably 3,000 men, many of them in dark combat fatigues— moved into central Vietnam's most handsome and historic city without detection. Emperor Gia Long had built a magnificent citadel there in 1802, diverting the waters of the River of Perfumes to fill the moats and erecting great brick walls— ninety feet thick at the main gates—to mark the boundaries of the capital city, the royal city and, in the heart of the fortress, the Forbidden City.

The French colonial governor had made his home in Hue. The city—off-limits to most American servicemen—had retained a French ambiance, with cream-colored buildings and red tile roofs, a large Catholic cathedral, a Jesuit school, nuns in habit in the hospitals and schools, even a sports club on the banks of the river. Sampans still poled its languid lagoons, and on lazy summer mornings it was possible to hear the thock-thock of tennis matches at Le Cèrcle Sportif.

Westmoreland had cabled Washington January 22 with a warning that the enemy might attempt a multibattalion attack on Hue, but the people of Hue didn't get the word. U.S. and Vietnamese intelligence officials celebrated Tet with a great feast in the back room of Hue's best Chinese restaurant, and some Americans were singing college songs and drinking toasts to the New Year as Viet Cong soldiers clambered into boats for an amphibious assault on the citadel.

With crack battalions of the North Vietnamese Army's 4th and 6th Regiments leading the way, enemy troops overran the city. The headquarters staff of the 1st ARVN division managed to hold out in the Peaceful Royal Library and a small temple in the northwest corner of the citadel, and a U.S. Army detachment on the south side of the Perfume River successfully threw back enemy attacks through the night. But at dawn, flying from the King's Knight, a 123-foot tower built in 1809 to fly the emperor's colors, was the red and blue banner of the Liberation Army.

The Viet Cong flag flew for twenty-five hard days . . .

"Breathing In"
From Dispatches
by Michael Herr
1977

For several decades before the 1960s, many smaller nations throughout Southeast Asia were involved in conflicts with neighboring nations. Vietnam was one such nation, so mired in conflict both internal and external that no one agreed on when these conflicts began. As early as the mid-1950s, small numbers of troops began trickling into Vietnam, each fighting for different nations and different ideologies. They were known as irregulars—soldiers who were not employed by a regular army but were hired for a specific purpose. They filtered into Vietnam acting as mercenaries for special interests eyeing Southeast Asia as some new frontier, the battleground over which the Cold War would be fought.

In this excerpt from his scathing book Dispatches, *former* Esquire *correspondent Michael Herr attempts to pinpoint the exact moment when Vietnam turned from a conflict run by irregulars into an "official" war run by nations.*

You couldn't find two people who agreed about when it began, how could you say when it began going off? Mission intellectuals like 1954 as the reference date; if you saw as far back as [World] War II and the Japanese occupation you were practically a historical visionary. "Realists" said that it began for us in 1961, and the common run of Mission flack insisted on 1965, post-Tonkin Resolution, as though all the killing that had gone before wasn't really war. Anyway, you couldn't use standard methods to date the doom; might as well say that Vietnam was where the Trail of Tears was headed all along, the turnaround point where it would touch and come back to form a containing perimeter; might just as well lay it on the proto-Gringos who found the New England woods too raw and empty for their peace and filled them up with their own imported devils. Maybe it was already over for us in Indochina when Alden Pyle's body washed up under the bridge at Dakao, his lungs all full of mud; maybe it caved

in with Dien Bien Phu. But the first happened in a novel, and
while the second happened on the ground it happened to the
French, and Washington gave it no more substance than if
Graham Greene had made it up too. Straight history, auto-
revised history, history without handles, for all the books
and articles and white papers, all the talk and the miles of
film, something wasn't answered, it wasn't even asked. We
were backgrounded, deep, but when the background started
sliding forward not a single life was saved by the information. The thing had transmitted too much energy, it heated
up too hot, hiding low under the fact-figure crossfire there
was a secret history, and not a lot of people felt like running
in there to bring it out.

One day in 1963 Henry Cabot Lodge was walking around
the Saigon Zoo with some reporters, and a tiger pissed on him
through the bars of its cage. Lodge made a joke, something
like, "He who wears the pee of the tiger is assured of success
in the coming year." Maybe nothing's so unfunny as an omen
read wrong.

Some people think 1963's a long time ago; when a dead
American in the jungle was an event, a grim thrilling novelty.
It was spookwar then, adventure; not exactly soldiers, not
even advisors yet, but Irregulars, working in remote places
under little direct authority, acting out their fantasies with
more freedom than most men ever know. Years later, leftovers
from that time would describe it, they'd bring in names like
Gordon, Burton, and Lawrence, elevated crazies of older
adventures who'd burst from their tents and bungalows to rub

up hard against the natives, hot on the sex-and-death trail, "lost to headquarters." There had been Ivy League spooks who'd gone bumbling and mucking around in jeeps and beat-up Citroens, Swedish K's across their knees, literally picnicking along the Cambodian border, buying Chinese-made shirts and sandals and umbrellas. There'd been ethnologue spooks who loved with their brains and forced that passion on the locals, whom they'd imitate, squatting in black pajamas, jabbering in Vietnamese. There had been one man who "owned" Long An Province, a Duke of Nha Trang, hundreds of others whose authority was absolute in hamlets or hamlet complexes where they ran their ops until the wind changed and their ops got run back on them. There were spook deities, like Lou Conein, "Black Luigi," who (they said) ran it down the middle with the VC, the GVN [Government of Vietnam], the Mission and the Corsican Maf; and Edward Landsdale himself, still there in '67, his villa a Saigon landmark where he poured tea and whiskey for second-generation spooks who adored him, even now that his batteries were dead. There were executive spooks who'd turn up at airstrips and jungle clearings sweating like a wheel of cheese in their white suits and neckties; bureau spooks who sat on dead asses in Dalat and Qui Nhon, or out jerking off in some New Life Village; Air America spooks who could take guns or junk or any kind of death at all and make it fly; Special Forces spooks running around in a fury of skill to ice Victor Charlie.

History's heavy attrition, tic and toc with teeth, the smarter ones saw it winding down for them on the day that

Lodge first arrived in Saigon and commandeered the villa of the current CIA chief, a moment of history that seemed even sweeter when you knew that the villa had once been headquarters of the Deuxieme Bureau. Officially, the complexion of the problem had changed (too many people were getting killed, for one thing), and the romance of spooking started to fall away like dead meat from a bone. As sure as heat rises, their time was over. The war passed along, this time into the hard hands of firepower freaks out to eat the country whole, and with no fine touches either, leaving the spooks on the beach.

They never became as dangerous as they'd wanted to be, they never knew how dangerous they really were. Their adventure became our war, then a war bogged down in time, so much time so badly accounted for that it finally became entrenched as an institution because there had never been room made for it to go anywhere else. The Irregulars either got out or became regular in a hurry. By 1967 all you saw was the impaired spook reflex, prim adventurers living too long on the bloodless fringes of the action, heartbroken and memory ruptured, working alone together toward a classified universe. They seemed like the saddest casualties of the Sixties, all the promise of good service on the New Frontier either gone or surviving like the vaguest salvages of a dream, still in love with their dead leader, blown away in his prime and theirs; left now with the lonely gift they had of trusting no one, the crust of ice always forming over the eye, the jargon stream thinning and trickling out: Frontier sealing, census grievance, black operations (pretty good, for jargon), revolutionary development, armed propaganda. I asked a spook what that one meant and he just smiled. Surveillance, collecting, and reporting, was like a carnival bear now, broken and dumb, an Intelligence beast, our own. And by late 1967, while it went humping and stalking all over Vietnam, the Tet Offensive was already so much incoming.

"The Secretary of the Army Regrets . . ." From **We Were Soldiers Once . . . and Young** *By Lt. Gen. Harold G. Moore and Joseph Galloway 1992*

The suffering endured during the war was not limited to those on the battlefield. One can argue that the pain of war is most harshly felt by the loved ones of those who are killed in battle. In "Death in the Ia Drang Valley," we saw firsthand the horror suffered in Ia Drang. In this excerpt from We Were Soldiers Once . . . and Young, *by Lt. Gen. Harold G. Moore and journalist Joseph Galloway, two men who survived the slaughter at Ia Drang, we begin to see the pain and suffering felt by those at home in the United States.*

Up until that point, the war had been very limited in its scope, and no single battle had caused major loss of life. The U.S. Army was unprepared for what happened in the Ia Drang Valley, and it did not have the resources to respectfully inform so many families that their husbands and sons had been killed. The army had to rely on the impersonal telegram—delivered by a cab driver—to convey its regrets on the death of a loved one. The fact that so many of these young families lived on military bases caused much concentrated pain since the young men who died in the battle of Ia Drang had all trained and gone over to Vietnam together. In this excerpt, we visit the incredibly tormenting moments of receiving a telegram from the U.S. Army once the bodies had been counted following Ia Drang.

————□————

The guns were at last silent in the valley. The dying was done, but the suffering had only just begun. The men of the 1st Cavalry Division had done what was asked of them. The Army field morgues were choked with the bodies of more than 230 soldiers wrapped in their green rubber ponchos. More than 240 maimed and wounded troopers moved slowly along the chain from battlefield aid station to medical clearing station to field hospital, and onto the ambulance transport planes.

Some whose wounds would heal soon enough for eventual return to duty in Vietnam were flown only as far as Army hospitals in Japan. The most seriously injured were flown to the Philippines; their conditions were stabilized at the hospital at Clark Field, and then they were loaded onto planes that would take them to military hospitals near their homes in the United States . . .

But on November 18, 1965, in the sleepy southern town of Columbus, Georgia, half a world away from Vietnam, the first of the telegrams that would shatter the lives of the innocents were already arriving from Washington. The war was so new and the casualties to date so few that the Army had not even considered establishing the casualty-notification teams that later in the war would personally deliver the bad news and stay to comfort a young widow or elderly parents until friends and relatives could arrive. In Columbus, in November and December 1965, Western Union simply handed the telegrams over to Yellow Cab drivers to deliver.

The driver who brought the message of the death in battle of Sergeant Billy R. Elliott, Alpha Company, 1st Battalion, 7th Cavalry, to his wife, Sara, was blind drunk and staggering. As Mrs. Elliott stood in the doorway of her tiny bungalow, clutching the yellow paper, the bearer of the bad tidings fell backward off her porch and passed out in her flower bed. Then the Army briefly lost her husband's body on its journey home.

When a taxi driver woke up the very young, and very pregnant Hispanic wife of a 1st Battalion trooper at 2 A.M. and held out the telegram, the woman fainted dead away. The driver ran next door and woke up the neighbors to come help. The new widow could not speak or read English, but she knew what that telegram said.

The knock on the door at the home of Sergeant Jeremiah (Jerry) Jivens of Charlie Company, 1st Battalion, 7th Cavalry, came at 4 A.M. Betty Jivens Mapson was fourteen at the time: "I have told this story before to friends about how the taxi drivers used to deliver the telegrams to families who'd lost loved ones over there. Today it almost sounds unbelievable. Luckily, my Mom's sister lived with us and was with her when the knock came at our door at 4 A.M. My Mom collapsed completely as this stranger handed the telegram to us. How cold and inhuman, I thought."

In Columbus that terrible autumn, someone had to do
the right thing since the Army wasn't organized to do it. For
the families of the casualties of the 1st Battalion, 7th
Cavalry, that someone was my wife, Julia Compton Moore,
daughter of an Army colonel, wife of a future Army general,
and mother of five small children, including two sons who
would follow me to West Point and the Army.

Julie talks of those days as a time of fear; a time when
the mere sight of a Yellow Cab cruising through a neighbor-
hood struck panic in the hearts of the wives and children of
soldiers serving in Vietnam. As the taxicabs and telegrams
spread misery and grief, Julie followed them to the trailer
courts and thin-walled apartment complexes and boxy bungalows, doing her best to comfort those whose lives had been
destroyed. Two of those widows she can never forget: The
widow of Sergeant Jerry Jivens, who received her with great
dignity and presence in the midst of such sorrow, and that
frightened young Hispanic widow, pregnant with a boy child
who would come into this world in March without a father.

When the coffins began arriving home, my wife attended
the funeral of all but one of the 1st Battalion, 7th Cavalry
troopers who were buried at the Fort Benning cemetery. The
first funeral at Benning for a 1st Battalion casualty was that
of Sergeant Jack Gell of Alpha Company. Julie turned on the
evening news, and there on television was the saddest sight
she had ever seen: one of my beloved troopers being buried
and Fort Benning had not notified her. She called Survivors
Assistance and told them in no uncertain terms that they
must inform her of every 1st Battalion death notification

and of every funeral for a 1st Battalion soldier at the post cemetery.

Julie recalls, "I was so fearful when I began calling on the widows I would be very unwelcome, because it was my husband who ordered their husbands into battle. I thought of a million reasons why I should not go, but my father called me and told me to go, so I went. They were so happy to see me and they were so proud of their husbands. That was a little something that they still had to hang onto. There were thirteen widows from the 1st Battalion still living in that little town."

The same duty for the dead of the 2nd Battalion, 7th Cavalry was done by Mrs. Frank Henry, wife of the battalion executive officer, and Mrs. James Scott, wife of the battalion sergeant major, since the battalion commander, Lieutenant Colonel Bob McDade, was a bachelor at that time.

Kornelia Scott's first visit was to the home of Mrs. Martin Knapp, widow of a sergeant in Delta Company, 2nd Battalion, to offer condolences and assistance.

"There was immense grief and bitterness. So immense, that one widow was bitter that her husband had been killed and mine only wounded. Names, addresses and faces became a blur, especially when we started attending the funerals at Ft. Benning in late November and early December," says Mrs. Scott.

Mrs. Harry Kinnard, wife of the commander of the 1st Cavalry Division, and many others went public with their criticism of the heartless taxicab telegrams, and the Army swiftly organized proper casualty notification teams consisting of a chaplain and an accompanying officer. Nobody intended for this cruelty to happen. Everyone, including the Army, was taken totally by surprise by the magnitude of the casualties that had burst on the American scene at LZ X-Ray and LZ Albany.

But even after the Army teams were formed and the procedure was changed, it was months before a Yellow Cab could travel the streets of Columbus without spreading fear and pain in its wake. My wife remembers: "In December a taxi driver carrying a couple of young lieutenants stopped at my house. I hid behind the curtains, thinking, If I don't answer the door I won't have to hear the bad news. Then I decided: 'Come on, Julie, face up to it.' I opened the door and he asked me for directions to some address and I just about fainted. I told him: 'Don't you ever do that to me again!' The poor man told me that he understood, that all the taxi drivers had hated that terrible duty."

Far to the north, in Redding, Connecticut, the village messenger, an elderly man, knocked hesitantly on the door of John J. and Camille Geoghegan. Although the telegram was addressed to Mrs. Barbara Geoghegan, wife of Lieutenant John Lance (Jack) Geoghegan, the messenger knew what it said and he knew that Jack Geoghegan was the only child of that family.

As the Geoghegans read the news, the messenger broke down, quivering and weeping and asking over and over again if there was anything he could do to help them. Before they could deal with their own grief, the Geoghegans first had to deal with his; they hugged and comforted the messenger and helped him pull himself together for the long trip back to town through the deepening gloom.

Barbara Geoghegan was away that day; she had gone to New Rochelle, New York, to stay with her husband's elderly aunt. The aunt's husband had died on this date two years earlier and the family thought someone should be there to comfort her on so tragic an anniversary. When the Geoghegans telephoned Barbara with the news, she was writing her ninety-third letter to Jack, a letter filled, as usual, with news of their baby daughter, Camille. The next morning, in the mailbox at home, she found Jack's last letter to her. He wrote, "I had a chance to go on R and R, but my men are going into action. I cannot and will not leave them now."

When Captain Tom Metsker left for Vietnam in August of 1965, his wife, Catherine, and baby daughter, Karen, fourteen months old, moved home to Indiana to be near her family. Tom's father was in the U.S. Foreign Service, stationed in Monrovia, Liberia. Catherine recalls: "I finally got a teaching job to occupy my time and save some money. The first day was to be Monday, November 15. On that Sunday night, November 14, I was sick with a cold and fever. How could I start my new job? The phone rang. It was my uncle: 'There is a telegram for you.' Probably a message from Tom's parents in Liberia, I thought. 'Open it and read it to me,' I told him. THE SECRETARY OF THE ARMY REGRETS TO INFORM YOU . . . Tom was dead."

CHAPTER THREE

CULTURE: THE WAR BACK HOME, 1968–1971

"We Are Mired in a Stalemate . . ."
By Walter Cronkite
From the CBS Evening News, February 27, 1968

Walter Cronkite, longtime anchor of the CBS Evening News and one of the most recognized newscasters in the history of television broadcasting, had a big influence on public opinion during the Vietnam War and beyond. As anchor of the CBS Evening News with Walter Cronkite from 1962 to 1981, he established a reputation as an honest and fatherly figure. The following transcription from a CBS broadcast shortly after the Tet Offensive gives voice to the growing sentiment across the United States that progress in the war had greatly stalled and optimism was rapidly fading.

Tonight, back in more familiar surroundings in New York, we'd like to sum up our findings in Vietnam, an analysis that must be speculative, personal, subjective. Who won and who lost in the great Tet Offensive against the cities? I'm not sure. The Vietcong did not win by a knockout, but neither did we.

The referees of history may make it a draw. Another standoff may be coming in the big battles expected south of the Demilitarized Zone. Khe Sanh could well fall, with a terrible loss in American lives, prestige and morale, and this is a tragedy of our stubbornness there; but the bastion no longer is a key to the rest of the northern regions, and it is doubtful that the American forces can be defeated across the breadth of the DMZ with any substantial loss of ground. Another standoff. On the political front, past performance gives no confidence that the Vietnamese government can cope with its problems, now compounded by the attack on the cities. It may not fall, it may hold on, but it probably won't show the dynamic qualities demanded of this young nation. Another standoff.

We have been too often disappointed by the optimism of the American leaders, both in Vietnam and Washington, to have faith any longer in the silver linings they find in the darkest clouds. They may be right, that Hanoi's winter-spring offensive has been forced by the Communist realization that they could not win the longer war of attrition, and that the Communists hope that any success in the offensive will improve their position for eventual negotiations. It would improve their position, and it would also require our realization, that we should have had all along, that any negotiations must be that—negotiations, not the dictation of peace terms. For it seems now more certain than ever that the bloody experience of Vietnam is to end in a stalemate. This summer's almost certain standoff will either end in real give-and-take negotiations or terrible escalation; and for every means we have to escalate, the enemy can match us, and that applies to invasion of the North, the use of nuclear weapons, or the mere commitment of one hundred, or two hundred, or three hundred thousand more American troops to the battle. And with each escalation, the world comes closer to the brink of cosmic disaster.

To say that we are closer to victory today is to believe, in the face of the evidence, the optimists who have been wrong in the past. To suggest we are on the edge of defeat is to yield to unreasonable pessimism. To say that we are mired in stalemate seems the only realistic, yet unsatisfactory, conclusion. On the off chance that military and political analysts are right, in the next few months we must test the enemy's intentions, in case this is indeed his last big gasp before negotiations. But it is increasingly clear to this reporter that the only rational way out then will be to negotiate, not as victors, but as an honorable people who lived up to their pledge to defend democracy, and did the best they could.

This is Walter Cronkite. Good night.

"A Visit to Chicago: Blood, Sweat, and Tears"
By Steve Lerner
From the Village Voice, September 5, 1968

As images of the war's barbarity sifted into America's consciousness, the antiwar movement began to gain incredible steam. The counterculture was at its peak across the nation in 1968, and America's youth began taking to the streets, staging protests for civil rights and especially against the war in Vietnam. Some of the country's most publicized antiwar demonstrations took place at the 1968 Democratic National Convention in Chicago, where the Democratic Party was to nominate its candidate for president. On one side of the convention was Eugene McCarthy, who said he wanted immediate withdrawal from the region. On the other side was Hubert H. Humphrey, who wanted to reduce the amount of troops in the region if the Paris peace talks were adhered to, which was similar to the plan President Johnson had been pursuing.

Counterculture figures such as William S. Burroughs, Hunter S. Thompson, and Allen Ginsberg milled about the crowds of protesters as tensions began to mount because convention organizers deployed hundreds of police officers to keep the massive antiwar rallies in check. Chicago mayor Richard Daley rallied his police force, armed with riot gear, ordering them to use force if necessary to keep the protesters at bay. Thousands of protesters gathered outside the hotels that housed the Democratic Convention, hoping to voice their opinion about the war in Vietnam. Then, something exploded. Allegations of unwarranted violence and brutality by police ran rampant. The demonstrators rallied, but the police beat them back. Hundreds were arrested or injured. Many of the clashes were televised and were played and replayed for years. The images struck a chord with a nation that was already having doubts about the country's continuing role in the Vietnam conflict. This account by Steve Lerner, a journalist with the Village Voice, captures the chaos and confusion of the three-day protest.

—■—

CHICAGO—At half past midnight last Tuesday, the occupants of Lincoln Park were stormed by the Chicago police. It was not the first day, nor was it to be the last, that the Old City— the Lincoln Park area—had come under attack. During the previous two nights the Mayor's ordinance to clear the park by 11 P.M. had been vigorously enforced with nightsticks and tear gas.

Around midnight on Tuesday, some 400 clergy, concerned local citizens, and other respectable gentry joined the Yippies, members of Students for a Democratic Society, and the National Mobilization Committee to fight for the privilege of remaining in the park. Sporting armbands decorated with a black cross and chanting pacifist hymns, the men of God exhorted their radical congregation to lay down their bricks and join in a non-violent vigil.

Having foreseen that they could only wage a symbolic war with "little caesar Daley," several enterprising clergymen brought with them an enormous wooden cross, which they erected in the midst of the demonstrators under a street lamp. Three of them assumed heroic poses around the cross, more reminiscent of the Marines raising the flag over Iwo Jima than any Christ-like tableau they may have had in mind.

During the half-hour interlude between the arrival of the clergy and the police attack, a fascinating debate over the relative merits of strict non-violence versus armed self-defense raged between the clergy and the militants. While the clergy was reminded that their members were "over 30, the opiate of the people, and totally irrelevant," the younger generation was warned that "by calling the police 'pigs' and fighting with them you become as bad as they are." Although the conflict was never resolved, everyone more or less decided to do his own thing. By then the demonstrators, some 800 strong, began to feel the phalanx of police which encircled the park moving in, even the most militant forgot his quibbles with "the liberal-religious sell-out" and began to huddle together around the cross.

When the police announced that the demonstrators had five minutes to move out before the park was cleared, everyone went into his individual kind of panic . . .

Everyone knew that Wednesday was going to be the big one. Rumors circulated among the police that a cop had been killed in Tuesday's "white-riot." The demonstrators had their own beef: not only had they been gassed and beaten, not only had one of their leaders, Tom Hayden, been arrested twice on tramped-up charges of inciting to riot, disorderly conduct, resisting arrest, and letting the air out of the tires of a police vehicle, but the police had also broken into their community centers up near Lincoln Park.

Finally, the demonstrators were also set on marching to the Amphitheatre where what they called the Convention of Death was going through the motions of nominating Hubert. Crossing the bridge from the park in front of the Hilton to the bandshell in the middle of Grant Park, demonstrators filed into their seats listening to the prophetic words of Bob Dylan's "The Times They Are A-Changing." The police had already surrounded the park, the National Guard held all the bridges

leading across the railroad tracks to Chicago's downtown Loop
area, and helicopters filled the skies like hungry mosquitoes.

The Mayor had been good enough to circulate the
announcement telling the demonstrators that they were wel-
come to stay at the bandshell all day and enjoy themselves,
but that no march on the convention would be tolerated. His
instructions, however, were apparently too subtle for his
henchmen who saw the demonstrators as the enemy and
couldn't wrestle the idea of a truce into their image.
Accordingly, when a demonstrator replaced the American flag
with revolutionary red, the police became incensed at the
unpatriotic slur and moved in to restore decency and the
American way of life. (Jerry Rubin, accused of "soliciting to
mob action" and out of jail on $25,000, says that one of the
demonstrators who claims to have taken part in the lowering
of the American flag was his personal bodyguard, assigned to
him by the Mobilization. The same young man later turned
out to be an under cover agent who had been keeping Rubin
under surveillance.)

Once outside the bandshell and onto the sidewalk of a
highway which runs through the park, the marchers were
immediately halted by a line of Guardsmen who blocked the
route. Seeing a confrontation emerging, hundreds of newsmen
rushed to the front of the line to be in on the action. Instead
they formed a protective barrier between the troops and the
demonstrators, a pattern which was to be repeated frequently
during the next two days. After hours of frustrating negotiations which led nowhere, the demonstrators moved in a block

toward one of the bridges which lead back to the Hilton. It too was barricaded with troops as were the next four bridges, where tear gas was used to keep the demonstrators from trying to break through.

Most of us got across the fifth bridge and joined the mule-drawn covered wagons of the Poor People's Campaign which were headed for the Hilton. Michigan Avenue, for the first time in anyone's memory, clearly belonged to the people. There was a sense of victory and momentum as the mob of some 8,000 to 10,000 people converged on the Hilton. Everyone was still sneezing and spitting from the gas, but they felt high at having outfoxed the police who had clearly meant to isolate them in the park or split them up before they got to the Hilton.

Across the street, the other half of the crowd was being squashed against the walls of the Hilton. The pressure was so great that a plate glass window shattered. Terrified demonstrators were pulled through the window by a *Life* correspondent and a sympathetic waitress who gave them instructions as to where they could hide. Within minutes police piled into the hotel to protect the clientele by beating the protesters senseless in the plush corridors of the Hilton.

Outside, demonstrators were being peeled off the wall one at a time, sprayed with mace, beaten, and occasionally arrested. More forays by the police into the park across from the hotel sent people headlong into trees. During one of these maneuvers I watched a medic throw himself over the bloody head of a demonstrator—like a GI clutching a live grenade to his gut. When I saw him emerge from the fracas, the medic's head was in a worse state than the patient's.

By 10 P.M. the National Guard had pinned one group in the park in front of the Hilton and pushed the other two groups north and south down Michigan Avenue. A paddy wagon was caught in one of the mobs and demonstrators started rocking it back and forth in an attempt to overturn it. A busload of police got to them before they succeeded.

Down the side streets groups of 50 to 100 demonstrators broke off from the main action to disrupt the town. They moved quickly, leaving a trail of overturned garbage and shattered glass in their wake. Chased by police, they would split up and reform with other groups. One contingent, calling itself the Flower Cong, was particularly well organized and effective. I was following them up State Street when I caught sight of a blonde girl, a member of the Resistance, whom I'd talked to earlier in the day. I caught up with her just as the street filled up with cops. We turned to run in opposite directions and I lost sight of her until it was all over. Having seen that the police had blocked both ends of the street, I took refuge in a drugstore with several others. When I came out she was trying to sit up in the street, blood soaking through her hair, running down her chin and neck, and collecting in her collar. A car stopped and offered to take her to the hospital, so I carried her over and laid her out in the back seat. The car owner wanted to put newspaper under her head so she wouldn't stain the seats.

My hotel was nearby so I decided to go up and get rid of my shirt which was covered with her blood. At the main entrance I was stopped by a security guard who wouldn't let me in. I showed him my key but he still refused. After two similar rebuttals I was finally allowed to sneak in the back entrance and up the service elevator. "We don't want you walking around the lobby like that," one of the hotel policemen advised me. Up in my room I turned on the tube just as Daley was being asked by an interviewer if there was any evidence of brutality. Outside my window I could hear screams. I opened the shades and leaned out as the police pinned a bunch of demonstrators against the wall of the hotel. From the window above me someone heaved a roll of toilet paper and screamed "Pigs." When the street cleared, four bodies were lying in the gutter. Daley's voice droned on about how he had received no indication of police brutality.

"What Did You Do in the Class War, Daddy?"
By James Fallows
From the Washington Monthly, October 1975

How is somebody chosen to go to war? In our present volunteer army, every one of the soldiers has volunteered to serve in the armed forces of the United States. During Vietnam, however, when more and more soldiers were needed because the war was such a long and enormous undertaking, a draft was instituted in order to fill the need for soldiers. One would think that this would be a simple procedure, as any able-bodied youth over the age of eighteen would be compelled to serve his country in a time of war. But the 1960s was a time of

*challenging rules set up by institutions, especially when the
institution was the United States government involved in a
questionable war.*

*The popularity of draft-dodging began to grow as the
war grew and became increasingly harder to justify. But there
were heavy tolls to pay if one was caught dodging the draft.
Still, there were legal ways to get out of the draft. James
Fallows, the author of the following article, legally evaded
the draft and did not have to serve in the army; neither did
many of his friends. In this poignant article, Fallows, an editor
and writer for the* Washington Monthly, *questions the reasons
why he was excluded from the draft. Did the fact that he went
to Harvard, as did most of his friends, have anything to do
with why he was not drafted? Was it the fact that he came
from the upper middle class?*

Many people think that the worst scars of the war years have
healed. I don't. Vietnam has left us with a heritage rich in possibilities for class warfare, and I would like to start telling
about it with this story:

In the fall of 1969, I was beginning my final year in college.
As the months went by, the rock on which I had unthinkingly
anchored my hopes—the certainty that the war in Vietnam
would be over before I could possibly fight—began to crumble.
It shattered altogether on Thanksgiving weekend when,
while riding back to Boston from a visit with my relatives, I
heard that the draft lottery had been held and my birthdate
had come up number 45. I recognized for the first time that,

inflexibly, I must either be drafted or consciously find a way to prevent it.

In the atmosphere of that time, each possible choice came equipped with barbs. To answer the call was unthinkable, not only because, in my heart, I was desperately afraid of being killed, but also because among my friends, it was axiomatic that one should not be "complicit" in the immoral war effort. Draft resistance, the course chosen by a few noble heroes of the movement, meant going to prison or leaving the country. With much the same intensity with which I wanted to stay alive, I did not want those things either. What I wanted was to go to graduate school, to get married, and to enjoy those bright prospects I had been taught that life owed me.

I learned quickly enough that there was only one way to get what I wanted. A physical deferment would restore things to the happy state I had known during the undergraduate years. The barbed alternatives would be put off. By the impartial dictates of public policy I would be free to pursue the better side of life.

Like many of my friends whose numbers had come up wrong in the lottery, I set about securing my salvation. When I was not participating in anti-war rallies, I was poring over the Army's code of physical regulations. During the winter and early spring, seminars were held in the college common rooms. There, sympathetic medical students helped us search for disqualifying conditions that we, in our many years of good health, might have overlooked. Although, on the doctors' advice, I made a half-hearted try at fainting spells, my only real possibility was beating the height and weight regulations. My normal weight was close to the cut-off point for an "underweight" disqualification, and, with a diligence born of panic, I made sure I would have a margin. I was six-feet-one-inch tall at the time. On the morning of the draft physical I weighed 120 pounds.

Before sunrise that morning I rode the subway to the Cambridge city hall, where we had been told to gather for shipment to the examination at the Boston Navy Yard. The examinations were administered on a rotating basis, one or two days each month for each of the draft boards in the area. Virtually everyone who showed up on Cambridge day at the Navy Yard was a student from Harvard or MIT.

There was no mistaking the political temperament of our group. Many of my friends wore red arm bands and stop-the-war buttons. Most chanted the familiar words, "Ho, Ho, Ho Chi Minh/NLF is Gonna Win." [The NLF is the National Liberation Front—the North Vietnamese army]. One of the things we had learned from the draft counselors was that disruptive behavior at the examination was a worthwhile political goal, not only because it obstructed the smooth operation of the "criminal war machine," but also because it might impress the examiners with our undesirable character traits. As we climbed into the buses and as they rolled toward the Navy Yard, about half of the young men brought the chants to a crescendo. The rest of us sat rigid and silent, clutching x-rays and letters from our doctors at home.

Inside the Navy Yard, we were first confronted by a young sergeant from Long Beach, a former surfer boy no older than the rest of us and seemingly unaware that he had an unusual situation on his hands. He started reading out instructions for the intelligence tests when he was hooted down. He went out to collect his lieutenant, who clearly had been through a Cambridge day before. "We've got all the time in the world," he said, and let the chanting go on for two or three minutes. "When we're finished with you, you can go, and not a minute before."

From that point on the disruption became more purposeful and individual, largely confined to those whose deferment strategies were based on anti-authoritarian psychiatric traits. Twice I saw students walk up to young orderlies—whose hands were extended to receive the required cup of urine—and throw the vial in the orderlies' faces. The orderlies looked up, initially more astonished than angry, and went back to towel themselves off. Most of the rest of us trod quietly through the paces, waiting for the moment of confrontation when the final examiner would give his verdict. I had stepped on the scales at the very beginning of the examination. Desperate at seeing the orderly write down 122 pounds, I hopped back on and made sure that he lowered it to 120. I walked in a trance through the rest of the examination, until the final meeting with the fatherly physician who ruled on marginal cases such as mine. I stood there in socks and underwear, arms wrapped around me in the chilly building. I knew as I looked at the doctor's face that he understood exactly what I was doing.

"Have you ever contemplated suicide?" he asked after he finished looking over my chart. My eyes darted up to his. "Oh, suicide—yes, I've been feeling very unstable and unreliable recently." He looked at me, staring until I returned my eyes to the ground. He wrote "unqualified" on my folder, turned on his heel, and left. I was overcome by a wave of relief, which for the first time revealed to me how great my terror had been, and by the beginning of the sense of shame which remains with me to this day.

It was, initially, a generalized shame at having gotten away with my deception, but it came into sharper focus later in the day. Even as the last of the Cambridge contingent was throwing its urine and deliberately failing its color-blindness tests, buses from the next board began to arrive. These bore the boys from Chelsea, thick, dark-haired young men, the white proles of Boston. Most of them were younger than us, since they had just left high school, and it had clearly never occurred to them that there might be a way around the draft. They walked through the examination lines like so many cattle off to slaughter. I tried to avoid noticing, but the results were inescapable. While perhaps four out of five of my friends from Harvard were being deferred, just the opposite was happening to the Chelsea boys.

We returned to Cambridge that afternoon, not in government buses but as free individuals, liberated and victorious. The talk was high-spirited, but there was something close to the surface that none of us wanted to mention. We knew now who would be killed . . .

We have not, however, learned the lesson of the day at the Navy Yard, or the thousands of similar scenes all across the country through all the years of the war. Five years later, two questions have yet to be faced, let alone answered. The first is why, when so many of the bright young college men opposed the war, so few were willing to resist the draft, rather than simply evade it. The second is why all the well-educated presumably humane young men, whether they opposed the war or were thinking fondly of A-bombs on Hanoi, so willingly took advantage of this most brutal form of class discrimination—what it signifies that we let the boys from Chelsea be sent off to die.

The "we" that I refer to are the mainly white, mainly well-educated children of mainly comfortable parents, who are now mainly embarked on promising careers in law, medicine, business, academics. What makes them a class is that they all avoided the draft by taking one of the thinking-man's routes to escape. These included the physical deferment, by far the smartest and least painful of all; the long technical appeals through the legal jungles of the Selective Service System; the more disingenuous resorts to conscientious objector status; and, one degree further down the scale of personal inconvenience, joining the Reserves or the National Guard. I am not talking about those who, on the one hand, submitted to the draft and took their chances in the trenches, nor, on the other hand, those who paid the price of formal draft resistance or exile.

That there is such a class, identifiable as "we," was brought home to me by comparing the very different fates of the different sorts of people I had known in high school and college. Hundreds from my high school were drafted, and nearly two dozen killed. When I look at the memorial roll of names, I find that I recognize very few, for they were mainly the anonymous Mexican-American (as they were called at the time) and poor whites I barely knew in high school and forgot altogether when I left. Several people from my high school left the country; one that I know of went to jail. By comparison, of two or three hundred acquaintances from college and afterwards, I can think of only three who actually fought in Vietnam. Another dozen or so served in safer precincts of the military, and perhaps five went through the ordeal of formal resistance. The rest escaped in one way or another . . . There are those who contend that the world has always worked this way, and perhaps that is true. The question is why, especially in the atmosphere of the late sixties, people with any presumptions to character could have let it go on.

Vietnam Veterans Against the War Statement
By John Kerry
Delivered to the Senate Committee on Foreign Relations, April 23, 1971

In this passionate address to the Senate Committee on Foreign Relations, former swift-boat officer John Kerry adamantly issues his statement against the war in Vietnam. Among Kerry's honors were a Silver Star, Bronze Star with Combat V, and three Purple Hearts. When Kerry returned to the United States, he cofounded the Vietnam Veterans of America and, on April 23, 1971, testified in front of the U.S. Senate Committee on Foreign Relations. By appearing before the Senate, Kerry put a new face on the Vietnam protest movement—that of the veteran. Kerry became the voice that had actually been there, not the college protester or celebrity dissenter, but a soldier who had witnessed the atrocities that both sides were committing and realized that he could not morally support the war.

———□———

I would like to talk on behalf of all those veterans and say that several months ago in Detroit we had an investigation at which over 150 honorably discharged, and many very highly decorated, veterans testified to war crimes committed in Southeast Asia. These were not isolated incidents but crimes committed on a day-to-day basis with the full awareness of officers at all levels of command. It is impossible to describe to you exactly what did happen in Detroit—the emotions in the room and the feelings of the men who were reliving their experiences in Vietnam. They relived the absolute horror of what this country, in a sense, made them do.

They told stories that at times they had personally raped, cut off ears, cut off heads, taped wires from portable telephones to human genitals and turned up the power, cut off limbs, blown up bodies, randomly shot at civilians, razed villages in fashion reminiscent of Ghengis Khan, shot cattle and dogs for fun, poisoned food stocks, and generally ravaged the country-side of South Vietnam in addition to the normal ravage of war and the normal and very particular ravaging which is done by the applied bombing power of this country.

We call this investigation the Winter Soldier Investigation. The term Winter Soldier is a play on words of Thomas

Paine's in 1776 when he spoke of the Sunshine Patriots and summertime soldiers who deserted at Valley Forge because the going was rough.

We who have come here to Washington have come here because we feel we have to be winter soldiers now. We could come back to this country, we could be quiet, we could hold our silence, we could not tell what went on in Vietnam, but we feel because of what threatens this country, not the reds, but the crimes which we are committing that threaten it, that we have to speak out . . .

In our opinion and from our experience, there is nothing in South Vietnam which could happen that realistically threatens the United States of America. And to attempt to justify the loss of one American life in Vietnam, Cambodia or Laos by linking such loss to the preservation of freedom, which those misfits supposedly abuse, is to us the height of criminal hypocrisy, and it is that kind of hypocrisy which we feel has torn this country apart.

We found that not only was it a civil war, an effort by a people who had for years been seeking their liberation from any colonial influence whatsoever, but also we found that the Vietnamese whom we had enthusiastically molded after our own image were hard put to take up the fight against the threat we were supposedly saving them from.

We found most people didn't even know the difference between communism and democracy. They only wanted to work in rice paddies without helicopters strafing them and bombs with napalm burning their villages and tearing their country apart. They wanted everything to do with the war, particularly with this foreign presence of the United States of America, to leave them alone in peace, and they practiced the art of survival by siding with whichever military force was present at a particular time, be it Viet Cong, North Vietnamese or American.

We found also that all too often American men were dying in those rice paddies for want of support from their allies. We saw first hand how monies from American taxes were used for a corrupt dictatorial regime. We saw that many people in this country had a one-sided idea of who was kept free by the flag, and blacks provided the highest percentage of casualties. We saw Vietnam ravaged equally by American bombs and search and destroy missions, as well as by Viet Cong terrorism—and yet we listened while this country tried to blame all of the havoc on the Viet Cong.

We rationalized destroying villages in order to save them. We saw America lose her sense of morality as she accepted very coolly a My Lai and refused to give up the image of American soldiers who hand out chocolate bars and chewing gum.

We learned the meaning of free fire zones, shooting anything that moves, and we watched while America placed a cheapness on the lives of orientals.

We watched the United States' falsification of body counts, in fact the glorification of body counts. We listened while month after month we were told the back of the enemy was about to break. We fought using weapons against "oriental human beings." We fought using weapons against those people which I do not believe this country would dream of using were we fighting in the European theater. We watched while men charged up hills because a general said that hill has to be taken, and after losing one platoon or two platoons they marched away to leave the hill for reoccupation by the North Vietnamese. We watched pride allow the most unimportant battles to be blown into extravaganzas, because we couldn't lose, and we couldn't retreat, and because it didn't matter how many American bodies were lost to prove that point, and so there were Hamburger Hills and Khe Sanhs and Hill 81s and Fire Base 6s and so many others.

Now we are told that the men who fought there must watch quietly while American lives are lost so that we can exercise the incredible arrogance of Vietnamizing the Vietnamese.

Each day to facilitate the process by which the United States washes her hands of Vietnam someone has to give up his life so that the United States doesn't have to admit something that the entire world already knows, so that we can't say that we have made a mistake. Someone has to die so that President Nixon won't be, and these are his words, "the first President to lose a war."

We are asking Americans to think about that because how do you ask a man to be the last man to die in Vietnam? How do you ask a man to be the last man to die for a mistake? . . . We are here in Washington to say that the problem of this war is not just a question of war and diplomacy. It is part and parcel of everything that we are trying as human beings to communicate to people in this country—the question of racism which is rampant in the military, and so many other questions such as the use of weapons; the hypocrisy in our taking umbrage at the Geneva Conventions and using that as justification for a continuation of this war when we are more guilty than any other body of violations of those Geneva Conventions; in the use of free fire zones, harassment interdiction fire, search and destroy missions, the bombings, the torture of prisoners, all accepted policy by many units in South Vietnam. That is what we are trying to say. It is part and parcel of everything.

An American Indian friend of mine who lives in the Indian Nation of Alcatraz put it to me very succinctly. He told me how as a boy on an Indian reservation he had watched television and he used to cheer the cowboys when they came in and shot the Indians, and then suddenly one day he stopped in Vietnam and he said, "my God, I am doing to these people the very same thing that was done to my people," and he stopped. And that is what we are trying to say, that we think this thing has to end.

We are here to ask, and we are here to ask vehemently, where are the leaders of our country? Where is the leadership? We're here to ask where are [Secretary of State Robert S.] McNamara, [Civilian Advisor Walter] Rostow, [National Security Advisor McGeorge] Bundy, [Deputy Secretary of Defense Roswell] Gilpatrick, and so many others? Where are they now that we, the men they sent off to war, have returned? These are the commanders who have deserted their troops. And there is no more serious crime in the laws of war. The Army says they never leave their wounded. The marines say they never even leave their dead. These men have left all the casualties and retreated behind a pious shield of public rectitude. They've left the real stuff of their reputations bleaching behind them in the sun in this country . . .

We wish that a merciful God could wipe away our own memories of that service as easily as this administration has wiped away their memories of us. But all that they have done and all that they can do by this denial is to make more clear than ever our own determination to undertake one last mission—to search out and destroy the last vestige of this barbaric war, to pacify our own hearts, to conquer the hate and fear that have driven this country these last ten years and more. And more. And so when thirty years from now our brothers go down the street without a leg, without an arm, or a face, and small boys ask why, we will be able to say "Vietnam" and not mean a desert, not a filthy obscene memory, but mean instead where America finally turned and where soldiers like us helped it in the turning.

"A Boy Who Was Just 'There Watching It and Making Up His Mind'"
by John Pekkanen
From Life, *May 15, 1970*

On May 4, 1970, armed U.S. Guardsmen were sent to regain control of the Kent State University campus from students demonstrating against the Vietnam War, specifically the bombing of Cambodia. An ROTC (Reserve Officers' Training Corps) building had just been burned to the ground and the Guardsmen were there to prevent more rioting at the Ohio university. A large student protest was staged that day, and tension grew to a boiling point. As the crowd pressed the authorities, the Guardsmen blindly fired more than sixty shots into the crowd of protesters. When the smoke cleared, four students had been killed and nine were wounded.

The following is an intimate portrait of one of the students who died that day. Life correspondent John Pekkanen captures the impact of an innocent life stolen during one of the darkest hours of the Vietnam era.

———□———

On the morning of the day Bill Schroeder died the alarm went off at 7 A.M. He slept through it and his roommate had to turn it off. At 8:15 he finally got up, dressed in the blue denim jacket his grandfather gave him and the orange bellbottoms he called his "Brian Jones pants" after the late member of the Rolling Stones. ("He owned every record the Stones ever made," a friend remembers.) Leaving his house at 603 Franklin Street, only a few blocks from the Kent State University campus, he drove to class. "I went with him," one of his five housemates said. "He was wearing a purple flower and a yellow flower in each lapel of his jacket. He joked that the purple flower was his Purple Heart." Crossing the campus, Bill found a spent tear gas canister. He picked it up and turned it over to a nearby National Guardsmen.

His first class was ROTC, compulsory for Bill because he had transferred to Kent State as a sophomore last fall on an ROTC scholarship. He ranked second among his ROTC classmates academically. "We used to kid him about it," his roommate said, "because ROTC isn't something very popular on campuses these days." But if the kidding bothered him it didn't show. "It wasn't like he had to choose. He was in ROTC and he didn't like Vietnam and Cambodia but if he had to go to Vietnam he would have gone." He once confided to Gene Pekarick, a close friend and fellow psychology major, that he strongly disagreed with another ROTC student who, in discussing a hypothetical military operation, suggested the way to succeed was to "go in there and wipe them out." "Bill was just disgusted by that. He said, 'What kind of mentality is that?' He hated the thought of this kind of senseless killing this guy talked about."

The burning of the Kent State ROTC building the preceding Saturday night had bothered him a lot. He mentioned it on Sunday when he called home to his parents in Lorain, Ohio, a steel town about 60 miles from Kent. He assured his parents that he was all right and planned to take advantage of the disturbances by staying inside and studying.

The rally had been scheduled for noon on Monday on the commons, a gently rolling area now fresh with the burst of spring. Bill and Gene met after class and instead of going to lunch began walking to the rally. "He went because he was curious to see it. He wasn't a participant and he wasn't just a bystander. He was open-minded. He went there to observe."

As they moved toward the commons there was an edge of confrontation in the air, but no expectation of violence. Bill had earlier told his roommate that he didn't like the prospect of going to class under martial law. But as he and Gene walked past some Guardsmen, Gene said, "I hope none of those guys have itchy fingers," and it was Bill who reassured him. "Don't worry about it. They don't even have clips in their rifles."

They mingled in the rally, along with some 1,000 other students, most of whom shared their frame of mind—curious and a bit angry, but not outraged. "Nobody seems to understand," a student said later, "we just wanted the Guard off our campus. They were making everything worse." The metallic voice of the Guard bullhorn ordered the rally to disperse. Rights of assembly were suspended, it declared, authoritatively, anonymously. "A jeep came up toward us. They kept telling us to disperse. We just scattered and in the confusion I momentarily lost sight of Bill," Gene recalls. "The kids were strung out all over the area."

A cluster of students soon collected, shouting "Pigs off campus" at the Guard. Some of them, perhaps no more that 20, lobbed stones and the Guard responded with tear gas. Students hurled canisters back. The Guard ran out of tear gas and confronted by a skirmish line of several hundred students, drew together to regroup. Bill was standing about 100 feet from the Guardsmen, between them and the main body of students, when the Guardsmen opened fire. According to Gene, Bill wasn't shouting at the Guard or throwing rocks at them.

Gene, like the others around him, hit the ground. "Some girls had fainted. I looked over and saw a girl lying on the ground. She wasn't moving. It looked like Allison [Allison Krause, one of the four students who died]. I didn't really know her but she went out with a guy down the hall from me. A beautiful, happy girl. Then my roommate came running down the hill shouting at me, 'Do you know who they shot?' I said I think they shot Allison. 'No. They shot your buddy.' I ran up the hill and three people were around Bill. A crowd had gathered and then people moved away to give him room. He was alive and was able to speak. He just said, 'Where's an ambulance?' His voice was weak, like a whisper. An ambulance was nearby but it took another injured student away. About 10 minutes later one came for Bill. As they put him on the stretcher, he moved his leg up to help them. When they drove away I didn't even think he was hurt that bad." Ten hours later the university news service issued a statement: "Schroeder, Wm. K., 19, sophomore, DEAD. Five minutes after arrival."

Tuesday morning, after the National Guard had ordered everyone off campus until further notice, Bill Schroeder's housemates on Franklin Street prepared to leave for home. A group of them came out on the front porch and refused to allow anyone to enter the house. "Don't use our names," one said, "Just say we were a family and one of us was killed."

One of them, who identified himself as Bill's roommate, had known him since junior high school in Lorain and lived a block from his home. Monday night he had gone to the county morgue to make a positive identification of Bill. "We did everything together. Took walks, played basketball. Bill was good

at everything he tried. He had a mind, I mean a real mind."
Their high school principal said the same. Bill had an A-minus
average at Lorain Senior High School and had the highest rating
in every attitude category from citizenship to attendance. At
Kent State his average was B-plus. "He wanted to get into
psychology," his roommate said. "He liked it here. We would
spend a lot of nights together just talking, sometimes to 4 or
5 in the morning. He told us once that he really wanted to be a
writer. He'd been writing poetry for the last few years but
he'd always hide it."

The boy spoke haltingly, unable at times to control his
trembling. "Make sure you say one thing if nothing else. Say
that Bill was not throwing rocks or shouting at the
Guardsmen. It would have never crossed his mind to do that.
He was there watching it and making up his own mind about
it and they shot him." Then Bill Schroeder's friends went
back into the house and began packing his clothes.

CHAPTER FOUR

POWER, AUTHORITY, AND GOVERNANCE: THE AMERICAN GOVERNMENT, 1971–1975

"Pentagon's Statistics Underscore Intensity of Cambodia Bombing"
From the New York Times, June 22, 1973

As the South Vietnamese government was trying to withstand Communist advances, the neighboring country of Cambodia was immersed in a civil war haunted by Communist leaders. The Cambodian Communists were known as the Khmer Rouge, and their leader, Pol Pot, is remembered as one of the most vicious and maniacal leaders the world has ever known. For years, this civil war raged in Cambodia with the Khmer Rouge eventually gaining support and resources from the Communist North Vietnamese. Once again the United States military stepped in to aid a nation in need in the face of Communist aggression.

Beginning in 1969, the United States began running massive bombing raids in the Cambodian countryside, desperately trying to weaken the grip of the Khmer Rouge. In 1969 alone, the United States military sent 3,600 bombing missions over Cambodia—all secret missions. By 1973,

more than 500,000 Cambodians had been killed from these
air raids. Cambodia eventually fell to Communism in 1975,
and the reign of the Khmer Rouge in Cambodia ranks as
one of the most disastrous in modern history. Scholars,
currently investigating mass graves in Cambodia, now esti-
mate Pol Pot's three-and-a-half-year reign led to the deaths
of approximately two million people.

Washington, June 21 (UPI)—In the five months since the sign-
ing of the Vietnam cease-fire, the United States has bombed
Cambodia as heavily as it did in the preceding three years,
according to Pentagon statistics just made public.

The statistics also showed that in the seven years of
war in Indochina, the United States bombed the territory
of its ally, South Vietnam, four times as hard as it did
North Vietnam.

Last night, the Defense Department declassified 12
pages of documents detailing, month by month, the number of
attacks flown and the tonnages of bombs dropped on each of
the four nations of Indochina. In the past, the department
released the total tonnages dropped each month, but declined
to break down the figures by countries.

The figures show how much the air war has increased in
Cambodia. In the three years before the January cease-fire,
American aircraft dropped 175,000 tons of bombs there, but in
March, April, and May of this year, 140,000 tons were
dropped on Cambodia.

The Pentagon has said the bombing this month is continuing at roughly the same rate as previously, so that by now the tonnage should have passed 175,000 tons. The rate, of 50,000 tons a month, compares with 36,000 tons dropped on North Vietnam last December, including the heavy B-52 raids of the Christmas period.

On the other hand, the statistics support official assertions of earlier years that the "protective-reaction" raids during the official bombing halt of 1968–1972 were not a cover for mass air attacks. During the 41-month halt, 4,580 tons of bombs were dropped on North Vietnam, for an average of 112 tons a month. By comparison, during the years of bombing since then the monthly average dropped on North Vietnam was 20,000 tons.

For reasons unexplained, the statistics failed to include the 1965 tonnages dropped by fighter-bombers, though the B-52 tonnages for that year were included.

Excluding the missing figures the United States dropped 3.2 million tons of bombs on South Vietnam during the entire war, 2.1 million tons on Laos and 840,000 tons on North Vietnam.

South Vietnam was struck twice as heavily as was Germany in World War II and North Vietnam about two-thirds as heavily. In World War II the allies dropped 2.7 million tons of bombs in Europe, including 1.4 million tons on Germany. They dropped 656,000 tons in the Pacific theater, including 161,000 tons on Japan.

"Tell Your Friends That We're People"
By Don Luce
From The Pentagon Papers, Vol. 5
1972

Don Luce became a prolific wartime journalist during the conflict in Vietnam. Luce drew controversy and was eventually discredited by the South Vietnamese after his exposé on Con Son, a United States–supported POW camp notorious for its inhumane treatment of Vietcong prisoners. In this essay, written before Luce was expelled from South Vietnam, the author sympathizes with the devastated Vietnamese people. Their land was ravaged by war, and their faith in the United States had all but vanished. The reigning sentiment in the rural areas of Vietnam was a strong resentment toward the American occupiers. This resentment would eventually lead many Vietnamese to join the National Liberation Front (NLF). They were surrounded by war, constantly bombarded by American air forces. Everyday life became a struggle for survival, and the NLF took advantage of this, feeding off the growing backlash against the United States.

———□———

In May 1971, I was ordered to leave Vietnam for "special reasons." I had taken two American Congressmen to the Tiger Cages of Con Son. Before leaving, I asked the Vietnamese with whom I worked to tell me what they would like me to say to my American friends.

"Tell your friends that we're people," they said. "We're not slants, slopes, gooks, or dinks. We're people!"

The Vietnamese feel that they have been presented by U.S. government officials and the news media for so long as statistics and kill ratios that Americans have forgotten that they are people with many of the same aspirations, dreams, and fears that we have. To many Americans, the Vietnamese have become the nonpeople.

How has this happened? In reading the Pentagon Papers I was struck by the fact that none of the writers of the different documents could speak, read, or write Vietnamese. We have never had an ambassador in Vietnam who could say "hello" in Vietnamese. Our decisionmakers have all had to depend on interpreters or the elite class of Vietnamese who speak English for their understanding of that country. The result has been that our officials have learned how the farm people and workers feel from the educated English-speaking community—something like learning about the farmers in Iowa and Nebraska from Harvard professors or about New York City dock workers from Smith College co-eds . . .

We have lost more than 50,000 American lives and $150 billion of our national wealth [in Vietnam]. Yet a few months of language study has never been required from our decisionmakers.

Often the Vietnamese see things differently than U.S. officials. For example:

—An NLF soldier enters a village, shoots at a U.S. spotter plane, and then runs away. The pilot of the plane sends a message to headquarters and the village is bombed or bombarded. I have discussed this with U.S. army officers.

They know the NLF soldiers usually leave the village immediately after shooting at the plane, but, one explained, the village is bombed so that "someday the villagers will learn if they allow Viet Cong in their village they're going to get bombed."

The villagers look at it differently. They were bombed by airplanes, they say, and only the Americans have airplanes. Therefore, as long as the Americans are there, they'll be bombed. The solution, as it appears to them, is to join the NLF.

—In the Ba Long An Peninsula of Quang Ngai province and other areas where the machine-gunning of farm people by U.S. planes has been most prevalent, the farmers have learned to stand still and point their heads at the airplanes so they will make a smaller target as the planes look down on them.

"We used to lie down," they explain. "But now we stand there and point our heads at the planes. Fewer people are killed that way."

American pilots explain that they could still hit the farmers, but the fact that they just stand there indicates that they have nothing to hide—they're not Viet Cong.

Ironically, the farmers have learned this "trick" from the NLF cadre.

Often the villagers are warned before the bombardment. U.S. government officials carefully explain to visitors how much care is taken to prevent innocent civilian casualties.

One method described as "surprisingly successful" by the U.S. Air Force is the "I told you so" approach. Super Skymaster planes drop leaflets or use air-recorded tapes from powerful loudspeakers over suspected NLF areas telling everyone to *Chieu Hoi*, or come to the side of the Saigon government. A 1971 press release (#4016) by the Directorate of Information, Headquarters Seventh Air Force, described the purpose of the psyops (psychological operations) leaflets this way:

The message also contains a warning. A warning of attacks by planes and artillery. As the psyops aircraft moves away U.S. Air Force, Republic of Vietnam Air Force, or Royal Australian Air Force fighter bombers blanket the area with a barrage of firepower. Before the smoke clears the psyops pilot returns with another tape message, promising more of the same to the survivors who do not rally. "This is why we call it the 'I told you so' approach," Lieutenant Loss said.

In Quang Ngai province of Central Vietnam, the American Division has used tape recordings from an airplane to warn the villagers. A plane flies over the village [and] a ten- or twenty-second tape tells the villagers to leave immediately. Tape number T7-21A-70, used in 1971, announces:

Attention citizens: You must leave this area immediately. There will be artillery and air strikes tomorrow morning. Evacuate to the east to avoid an accident. There will be artillery and air strikes tomorrow morning. Evacuate to the east.

If there are NLF in the village, they pick up their guns and leave. Or, as some of the refugees say, the NLF soldiers stay and help the people to pack—perhaps discussing the cruelty of the Americans in making them move!

The villagers gather together their buffalo, pigs, chickens, rice, and children. Then the grandparents refuse to leave.

"We've lived here for seventy years," the old people say. "Our parents lived here and are buried here. We will not leave the graves of the ancestors."

And the only way that the family can get the grandparents to leave is to tell them that if they don't the grandchildren will be killed.

The family leaves the coconut trees, the rice fields, and the graves of the ancestors—all those things that have held the family together and been meaningful. The rice-planting songs and the evening stories told by Grandfather about days gone by are replaced by the thud of bombs. The people are crowded into the city slums and around the air bases. Their houses, if they have any, are built of cardboard, U.S. government cement and tin, or artillery-shell packing boxes. The bewildered, apathetic people sit in front of these dwellings staring at the ground. The six-cent-a-day refugee payments are held up by bureaucracy, or never come at all.

But the Vietnamese are a resilient people. They survive.

The men who once plowed the acre or two of rice land join one army or the other . . .

The United States has made more "Viet Cong" than it has killed. When a farmer's tomatoes or papaya are defoliated, that farmer becomes more sympathetic to the NLF. When families are forced to leave their homes and the burial grounds of their ancestors, they hate the people who move them. The lack of understanding of the Vietnamese and the disregard for Vietnamese life expressed throughout the Pentagon Papers has been militarily self-defeating.

For example, the United States forced the farm people into the refugee camps in order to deprive the NLF of food, intelligence, and personnel. But by placing so many people sympathetic to the NLF right in the middle of city slums, the NLF had a base of operations during the 1968 Tet Offensive. Guns and ammunition were brought into Saigon prior to the Tet Offensive in mock funerals. The "coffins" were buried in the cemeteries, where the refugees had been forced to build their shacks because of lack of any other space. The NLF soldiers moved in with friends, relatives, and sympathizers just prior to Tet. And while the children lit firecrackers, the men test-fired their rifles. When the offensive began there were plenty of refugees to show them the police stations and act as guides through the alleyways that form the jungles of Saigon.

The NLF made a misjudgment too. In their offensive, they did not expect that the Allies would bomb the Allied cities. "We just did not expect that the United States would bomb Saigon, Hue, and the other cities," I was told by one NLF official. The U.S. major who said about Ben Tre, "It became necessary to destroy the town to save it," was describing in a very real sense what has happened to all of Vietnam. To the military, there was no other alternative.

An Editorial from the New York Times, *June 21, 1971*

The Pentagon Papers—the secret government study of decision making about the Vietnam War—gave us an extraordinary look at how and why the Vietnam conflict escalated so dramatically throughout the years leading to Richard Nixon's presidency. Robert S. McNamara, who served as secretary of defense from 1961 to 1968 under Presidents Kennedy and Johnson, commissioned this top secret study on U.S. decision making about the war. The study, which became known as the Pentagon Papers, was completed in 1969 and consisted of forty-seven volumes and about 7,000 pages. Copies of the report were strictly controlled. Daniel Ellsberg, a civilian employee of the Department of Defense who worked on the project, was convinced that the war was wrong and leaked the papers to the New York Times. *Reporter Neil Sheehan prepared a series of lengthy articles, and the newspaper began the publication of the secret documents on June 13, 1971. After the third installment in the* Times, *the U.S. Department of Justice obtained a restraining order, forcing the newspaper to halt publication of the Pentagon Papers, citing that doing so would cause "immediate and irreparable harm" to the U.S. war effort. That started an extraordinary federal court battle that pitted the U.S. government against the press. The following editorial appeared in the* Times *during the fifteen-day halt of publishing the Pentagon Papers. The editorial attempts to justify publication of the papers, citing that the public was left in the dark on many aspects of the war.*

Ultimately, the U.S. Supreme Court ruled in a 6–3 decision that the government could not stop the Times *from publishing the Pentagon Papers. The landmark decision set a precedent for freedom of the press in the United States and fed the growing resentment toward the U.S. government and involvement in Vietnam. The Pentagon Papers revealed many controversial aspects of the war that were previously considered top secret. Most notably, the papers uncovered the extent of the military campaign prior to 1964, when involvement in Vietnam was first publicly revealed. Ultimately, the release of the papers caused great embarrassment to the Nixon administration. Today, the Pentagon Papers remain an important piece to the Vietnam saga, as the American public and press were able to question the authority and actions of the U.S. government.*

———□———

On November 25, 1964, some three weeks after President Johnson's election, The Times observed editorially that "another Vietnam reassessment is under way . . . [and] if there is to be a new policy now, if an Asian war is to be converted into an American war, the country has a right to insist that it be told what has changed so profoundly in the last two months to justify it." The country was not told.

Six months later, after repeated demands for "a straightforward explanation" of what was clearly becoming a major land war on the continent of Asia, this newspaper noted that "there is still no official explanation offered for a move that fundamentally alters the character of the American involvement in Vietnam" and pleaded "for the President to take the country into his confidence . . ."

These comments illustrate how Congress and the American people were kept in the dark about fundamental policy decisions affecting the very life of this democracy during the most critical period of the war. The conviction even then that the Government was not being frank with the American people has been fully confirmed by the massive Pentagon history and documentation which The Times began to publish last week—until the Government undertook to censor it.

The running commentary and documents that did appear in this newspaper before the Government moved to block them throw a clear spotlight on the decision-making process during the period up to and including the major escalation of the Vietnam War in 1964 and 1965. The multi-volume study on which The Times' account was based shows beyond cavil how the decisions affecting American participation in and conduct of the war were planned and executed while their far-reaching political effect and profound significance, fully appreciated at the top reaches of government, were either deliberately distorted or withheld altogether from the public.

Even more important, the papers as published thus far suggest that almost no one in the upper ranks of the Administration during this crucial period six and seven years ago was probing into the basic political issue on which the military operation depended: Was the Saigon Government's control of South Vietnam of such vital, long-range interest to the United States that it warranted an open-ended American military involvement—or was this really an unexamined conclusion that had already become an article of faith? Nearly every official concerned was discussing the tactics and strategy of the war, how to handle it, how to win it, how to come out of it, what plans to make under various contingencies. These were important matters indeed and the officials in question would not have been doing their duty if they had failed to consider them. They should not be faulted for this; nor was it in any way improper to have planned for every conceivable military eventuality.

But the missing factor was discussion or argumentation over the *raison d'être* of the war and the rationale for continuing massive American involvement in it. It seems to have been accepted without question by virtually everyone in the top ranks, except Under Secretary of State George Ball, that the interests of the United States did indeed lie, at almost any cost and overriding almost any risk, in military victory for the South Vietnamese Government even to the point of major American participation in a war on the land mass of Southeast Asia.

This was the premise, this the context, and this the fateful error. If, as the principal officers of the Government saw the country being drawn into such a war, a full and frank debate and discussion in Congress and outside had been undertaken, it is quite possible that events would have moved in a different way. No one will ever know, for this "open covenant, openly arrived at" between American Government and American people never materialized.

This, then, is what the Vietnam Papers prove—not venality, not evil motivation, but rather an arrogant disregard for the Congress, for the public, and for the inherent obligation of the responsibilities of leadership in a democratic society. The papers are not only part of the historical record; they are an essential part of that record. They are highly classified documents and so is the analytical study on which The Times' running commentary was based. But they carry the story of Vietnam no farther than 1968—now three years ago; they in no way affect current plans, operations, or policy; and there seems no longer any justification for these papers—along with many others in governmental files—to bear the classification that keeps them from general public access. Overclassification and misclassification of documents is at best a normal reflection of governmental inertia; but, as here, it is often used to conceal governmental error.

The material was not published by The Times for purposes of recrimination or to establish scapegoats or to heap blame on any individual in civilian or military ranks. It was published because the American public has a right to have it and because when it came into the hands of The Times, it was its function as a free and uncensored medium of information to make it public. This same principle held for The Washington Post when it too obtained some of the papers. To have acted otherwise would have been to default on a newspaper's basic obligation to the American people under the First Amendment, which is precisely the point that Federal District Judge Murray Gurfein suggested in his memorable decision in this newspaper's favor last Saturday.

And yet the Government of the United States, in an action unprecedented in modern American history, sought and is continuing to seek to silence both The New York Times and The Washington Post, claiming that "irreparable injury" to the national security would be caused by publication of further chapters in the Vietnam study. The fact is that "irreparable injury" has been done to the Government itself, not because of anything that has been published but, quite the contrary, because of the extraordinary action the Government took to thwart and subvert in this manner the constitutional principle of freedom of the press which is the very essence of American democracy. Judge Gurfein's decision—whether or not it is sustained on appeal—surely represents a landmark in the endless struggle of free men and free institutions against the unwarranted exercise of governmental authority.

From Abuse of Power
Edited by Stanley I. Kutler
1997

From February 1971 until July 1973, President Richard Nixon secretly tape-recorded thousands of private conversations with aides and public figures. Forty hours' worth of those tapes were released in April 1974. The resulting public tumult contributed to the president's resignation four months later, following the Watergate scandal.

In these excerpts from the tapes, we see how Nixon wanted to exploit the Pentagon Papers in his favor and how he wanted to get even with Daniel Ellsberg, the former aide who had leaked the papers to the press. Ellsberg, along with many others, would become a target for President Nixon, who was becoming increasingly paranoid and embarrassed with the state of the war in Vietnam. These excerpts from the so-called Nixon tapes capture the president speaking frankly to aides shortly after the New York Times *began publishing the Pentagon Papers.*

JUNE 17, 1971: THE PRESIDENT, [White House Chief of Staff H. R.] HALDEMAN, [Assistant for Domestic Affairs John Daniel] EHRLICHMAN, AND [Secretary of State Henry] KISSINGER, 5:17–6:13 P.M., OVAL OFFICE

A few days after the publication of the Pentagon Papers, Nixon discusses how to exploit the situation to his advantage. He is interested in embarrassing the Johnson administration on the bombing halt, for example. Here, he wants a break-in at the Brookings Institution, a centrist Washington think tank, to find classified documents that might be in the Brookings safe.

———◻———

HALDEMAN: You maybe can blackmail [Lyndon B.] Johnson on this stuff [Pentagon Papers].

PRESIDENT NIXON: What?

HALDEMAN: You can blackmail Johnson on this stuff and it might be worth doing . . . The bombing halt stuff is all in that same file or in some of the same hands . . .

PRESIDENT NIXON: Do we have it? I've asked for it. You said you didn't have it.

HALDEMAN: We can't find it.

KISSINGER: We have nothing here, Mr. President.

PRESIDENT NIXON: Well, damnit, I asked for that because I need it.

KISSINGER: But Bob and I have been trying to put the damn thing together.

HALDEMAN: We have a basic history in constructing our own [file on Vietnam], but there is a file on it.

PRESIDENT NIXON: Where?

HALDEMAN: [Presidential aide Tom Charles] Huston swears to God there's a file on it and it's at Brookings [Institution].

PRESIDENT NIXON: . . . Bob? Bob? Now do you remember Huston's plan [for White House–sponsored break-ins as part of domestic counter-intelligence operations]? Implement it.

KISSINGER: . . . Now Brookings has no right to have classified documents.

PRESIDENT NIXON: . . . I want it implemented . . . Goddamnit, get in and get those files. Blow the safe and get it.

HALDEMAN: They may very well have cleaned them by now but this thing, you need to—

KISSINGER: I wouldn't be surprised if Brookings had the files.

HALDEMAN: My point is Johnson knows that those files are around. He doesn't know for sure that we don't have them around.

JUNE 24, 1971: THE PRESIDENT, HALDEMAN, AND [Press Secretary Ron] ZIEGLER, 9:38–10:09 A.M., OVAL OFFICE

In the wake of the Pentagon Papers revelations, Nixon demanded that someone coordinate a scheme for declassifying older documents, dating back to World War II and Korea, as well as Vietnam. While he was furious about the leak of the Pentagon Papers, he plans his own leak to reveal embarrassing failures or shortcomings in foreign policies under his predecessors. He wants his own "Ellsberg who's on our side."

———□———

PRESIDENT NIXON: God, wait until these World War II things come out now we've got—I've got some more—done some more thinking on that. We've got to get a better team on it . . .

HALDEMAN: That's right.

PRESIDENT NIXON: It will have to take about twelve guys under somebody a little bit more responsible, but [Tom Charles Huston's] a son of a bitch. I mean, Bob, you get all this stuff. Do you realize that? We can get it all.

HALDEMAN: Yeah.

PRESIDENT NIXON: Well, we're going to expose them. God, Pearl Harbor and the Democratic party will—they'll have gone without a trace if we do this correctly. Who would you put in charge, Bob?

HALDEMAN: That's what I'm trying to figure because—

PRESIDENT NIXON: You've got [Special Counsel Charles] Colson doing too much, but he's the best. It's the Colson type of man that you need . . . It will be very good to have somebody who knew the subject. I mean, what you really need is an [Daniel] Ellsberg, an Ellsberg who's on our side; in other words, an intellectual who knows the history of the times, who knows what he's looking for.

HALDEMAN: Okay. Well, then I know who to go to.

PRESIDENT NIXON: Yeah. Who would you use?

HALDEMAN: [National Security aide] Dick Allen.

PRESIDENT NIXON: That's the guy. Allen's the guy. Put him in charge of it. He's the—you've got it named. That's exactly the man I want . . . We just desperately need, I think, we need this guy, this declassification thing.

HALDEMAN: Dick Allen is the guy to do it. He's exactly what we're talking about. Why all the sophistication—

PRESIDENT NIXON: I want Huston in on the team.

HALDEMAN: All right.

PRESIDENT NIXON: Because Huston will know what to look for. He knows a lot about intelligence . . .

ZIEGLER: Allen will do a good job at this.

PRESIDENT NIXON: No. This guy is—don't go back to World War II, this first. The first things I want to go back to—I want to go to the Cuban missile crisis and I want to go to the Bay of Pigs.

HALDEMAN: We, those are the ones that are most likely to get lost the fastest . . . World War II stuff we can always get.

PRESIDENT NIXON: People are being—probably burning stuff and hiding stuff as fast as they can. A lot of this stuff will be gone. The bombing halt story, incidentally, is run into the

Ellsberg thing and I think it's now time to get that out if it's any good for us.

HALDEMAN: Okay. Well, we got, as I told you, we've got that except Huston says there's three segments yet that aren't complete, but he's got the raw material. He can complete them . . .

JUNE 29, 1971: THE PRESIDENT AND [CHARLES] COLSON, 2:28–2:32 P.M., THE WHITE HOUSE TELEPHONE

The following two conversations reveal some of the president's responses to Daniel Ellsberg, the man who leaked the Pentagon Papers, and to Nixon's enemies in the foreign-policy establishment.

PRESIDENT NIXON: If you can get him [Daniel Ellsberg] tied in with some communist groups, that would be good. Jay [Lovestone, ex-Communist, then a prominent AFL-CIO official] thinks he is but, of course, that's my guess that he's in with some subversives, you know.

JUNE 30, 1971: THE PRESIDENT, [Attorney General John] MITCHELL, AND KISSINGER, 2:55–3:07 P.M., OVAL OFFICE

PRESIDENT NIXON: Well, I want to get that out . . . Don't worry about his [Ellsberg's] trial. Just get everything out. Try him in the press. Try him in the press. Everything, John, that there is on the investigation get it out, leak it out. We want to destroy him in the press. Press. Is that clear?

JULY 1, 1971: THE PRESIDENT, HALDEMAN, AND KISSINGER, 8:45–9:52 A.M., OVAL OFFICE

Within a week after the publication of the Pentagon Papers, the president had authorized the creation of a secret, special White House investigative unit to "stop security leaks and to investigate other sensitive security matters." Thus, Nixon called into being the "Plumbers," headed by Egil Krogh and David Young, and including E. Howard Hunt and G. Gordon Liddy. For Nixon, the Plumbers was his means of matching the tactics of his enemies and the deviousness of their conspiracy against him. On July 1, Colson asked Hunt in a telephone conversation, "Should we go down the line to nail the guy [Daniel Ellsberg] cold?" Hunt replied in the affirmative. Earlier that day, Nixon elaborated on his other counterattacks against leakers, drawing on his experience in the Alger Hiss case. [As a young congressman in 1948, Nixon rallied public support against Hiss, a former State Department official who leaked sensitive material to the former Soviet Union].

———□———

PRESIDENT NIXON: Here's what I have in mind and I've got to get [Tom Charles] Huston or somebody fast, but either Huston or somebody like Huston fast. That's why the, you know, the Dick Allen thing. I think you've got to take Dick Allen on the mountaintop and see if he wants to handle this.

HALDEMAN: Who said that he didn't?

PRESIDENT NIXON: You didn't think he was the right guy. You wanted somebody that—John [Ehrlichman] didn't, I think, or somebody because he's too—

HALDEMAN: Well, Dick doesn't think he is . . .

PRESIDENT NIXON: . . . This is what I want. I have a project that I want somebody to take it just like I took the Hiss case, the [Elizabeth] Bentley case, and the rest. . . . And I'll tell you what. This takes—this takes 18 hours a day. It takes devotion and dedication and loyalty and diligence such as you've never seen, Bob. I've never worked as hard in my life and I'll never work as hard again because I don't have the energy. But this thing is a hell of a great opportunity because here is what it is. I don't have direct knowledge of who the Goddamn leaker is and, you see—and here's where John will recall I don't—probably we don't have to tell him.

You probably don't know what I meant when I said yesterday that we won the Hiss case in the papers. We did. I had to leak stuff all over the place. Because the Justice Department would not prosecute it. [J. Edgar] Hoover didn't even cooperate . . . It was won in the papers. John Mitchell doesn't understand that sort of thing. He's a good lawyer. It's hard to him. John Ehrlichman will have difficulty. But what I mean is we have to develop now a program, a program for leaking out information. We're destroying these people in the papers. That's one side of it. Had a gap in the conspiracy.

The other side of it is the declassification. Declassification. And then leaking to or giving up to our friends the stories that they would like to have such as the Cuban [invasion]. Do you know what I mean? Let's have a little fun. Let me tell you what the declassification [of other administrations' papers] in previous years that helps us. It takes the eyes off of Vietnam. It gets them thinking about the past rather than our present problems. You get the point.

HALDEMAN: Yeah. Absolutely . . .

PRESIDENT NIXON: . . . Now do you see what we need? I need somebody . . . I wish you could get a personality type, oh, like [John C.] Whitaker who will work his butt off and do it honorably. I really need a son of a bitch like Huston who will work his butt off and do it dishonorably. Do you see what I mean? Who will know what he's doing and I want to know, too. And I'll direct him myself. I know how to play this game and we're going to start playing it.

"Peace with Honor"
Address by President Richard M. Nixon
January 23, 1973

On January 23, 1973, after nearly five years of talks, negotiators Henry Kissinger of the United States and Le Duc Tho of North Vietnam signed a peace agreement to end the war in Vietnam. President Nixon announced the Paris Peace Accords that evening on national television and radio, praising it as the fulfillment of his promise to bring "peace with honor" to Vietnam. On January 27, representatives of the United States, North and South Vietnam, and the Vietcong signed the peace agreement, officially ending America's involvement in the

Vietnam War. The agreement's key provisions included a cease-fire throughout Vietnam, the withdrawal of U.S. forces, the release of prisoners of war, and the reunification of North and South Vietnam through peaceful means. The treaty also stated that the South Vietnamese government was to remain in place until new elections were held, and North Vietnamese forces in the south were not to be reinforced nor advance further. Although U.S. involvement would remain minimal, the war would rage on for two more years until the South finally fell to North Vietnam.

———□———

Good evening. I have asked for this radio and television time tonight for the purpose of announcing that we today have concluded an agreement to end the war and bring peace with honor in Vietnam and in Southeast Asia.

The following statement is being issued at this moment in Washington and Hanoi:

At 12:30 Paris time today [Tuesday], January 23, 1973, the Agreement on Ending the War and Restoring Peace in Vietnam was initialed by Dr. Henry Kissinger on behalf of the United States, and Special Adviser Le Duc Tho on behalf of the Democratic Republic of Vietnam.

The agreement will be formally signed by the parties participating in the Paris Conference on Vietnam on January 27, 1973, at the International Conference Center in Paris.

The cease-fire will take effect at 2400 Greenwich Mean Time, January 27, 1973. The United States and the Democratic

Republic of Vietnam express the hope that this agreement will insure stable peace in Vietnam and contribute to the preservation of lasting peace in Indochina and Southeast Asia.

That concludes the formal statement.

Throughout the years of negotiations, we have insisted on peace with honor. In my addresses to the Nation from this room of January 25 and May 8 [1972], I set forth the goals that we considered essential for peace with honor.

In the settlement that has now been agreed to, all the conditions that I laid down then have been met. A cease-fire, internationally supervised, will begin at 7 P.M., this Saturday, January 27, Washington time. Within 60 days from this Saturday, all Americans held prisoners of war throughout Indochina will be released. There will be the fullest possible accounting for all of those who are missing in action.

During the same 60-day period, all American forces will be withdrawn from South Vietnam.

The people of South Vietnam have been guaranteed the right to determine their own future, without outside interference.

By joint agreement, the full text of the agreement and the protocols to carry it out, will be issued tomorrow.

Throughout these negotiations we have been in the closest consultation with President [Nguyen Van] Thieu and other representatives of the Republic of Vietnam. This settlement meets the goals and has the full support of President Thieu and the Government of the Republic of Vietnam, as well as that of our other allies who are affected.

The United States will continue to recognize the Government of the Republic of Vietnam as the sole legitimate government of South Vietnam.

We shall continue to aid South Vietnam within the terms of the agreement and we shall support efforts by the people of South Vietnam to settle their problems peacefully among themselves.

We must recognize that ending the war is only the first step toward building the peace. All parties must now see to it that this is a peace that lasts, and also a peace that heals, and a peace that not only ends the war in Southeast Asia, but contributes to the prospects of peace in the whole world.

This will mean that the terms of the agreement must be scrupulously adhered to. We shall do everything the agreement requires of us and we shall expect the other parties to do everything it requires of them. We shall also expect other interested nations to help insure that the agreement is carried out and peace is maintained.

As this long and very difficult war ends, I would like to address a few special words to each of those who have been parties in the conflict.

First, to the people and Government of South Vietnam: By your courage, by your sacrifice, you have won the precious right to determine your own future and you have developed the strength to defend that right. We look forward to working with you in the future, friends in peace as we have been allies in war.

To the leaders of North Vietnam: As we have ended the war through negotiations, let us now build a peace of reconciliation. For our part, we are prepared to make a major effort to help achieve that goal. But just as reciprocity was needed to end the war, so, too, will it be needed to build and strengthen the peace.

To the other major powers that have been involved even indirectly: Now is the time for mutual restraint so that the peace we have achieved can last.

And finally, to all of you who are listening, the American people: Your steadfastness in supporting our insistence on peace with honor has made peace with honor possible. I know that you would not have wanted that peace jeopardized. With our secret negotiations at the sensitive stage they were in during this recent period, for me to have discussed publicly our efforts to secure peace would not only have violated our understanding with North Vietnam, it would have seriously harmed and possibly destroyed the chances for peace. Therefore, I know that you now can understand why, during these past several weeks, I have not made any public statements about those efforts.

The important thing was not to talk about peace, but to get peace and to get the right kind of peace. This we have done.

Now that we have achieved an honorable agreement, let us be proud that America did not settle for a peace that would have betrayed our allies, that would have abandoned our prisoners of war, or that would have ended the war for us but would have continued the war for the 50 million people of Indochina. Let us be proud of the 2 1/2 million young Americans who served in Vietnam, who served with honor and distinction in one of the most selfless enterprises in the history of nations. And let us be proud of those who sacrificed, who gave their lives so that the people of South Vietnam might live in freedom and so that the world might live in peace.

In particular, I would like to say a word to some of the bravest people I have ever met—the wives, the children, the families of our prisoners of war and the missing in action. When others called on us to settle on any terms, you had the courage to stand for the right kind of peace so that those who died and those who suffered would not have died and suffered in vain, and so that, where this generation knew war, the next generation would know peace. Nothing means more to me at this moment than the fact that your long vigil is coming to an end.

Just yesterday, a great American, who once occupied this office, died. In his life President [Lyndon B.] Johnson endured the vilification of those who sought to portray him as a man of war. But there was nothing he cared about more deeply about than achieving a lasting peace in the world.

I remember the last time I talked with him. It was just the day after New Year's. He spoke then of his concern with bringing peace, with making it the right kind of peace, and I was grateful that he once again expressed his support for my efforts to gain such a peace. No one would have welcomed this peace more than he.

And I know he would join me in asking for those who died and for those who live, let us consecrate this moment by resolving together to make the peace we have achieved a peace that will last.

Thank you and good evening.

"The Fall of Saigon, April, 1975"
By unknown author

*History shows that the "Peace with honor" speech and
Paris Peace Accords were merely a way for the United
States to extract itself from Vietnam with some form of dignity.
Within weeks of the American departure, the Communists
violated the cease-fire, and by early 1974, the war had
resumed. By the end of 1974, South Vietnamese authorities
reported that altogether 80,000 people had been killed in
fighting during the year, making it the deadliest year of the
Vietnam War. On April 30, 1975, the last few Americans
still in South Vietnam were airlifted out of the country as
the South Vietnamese capital of Saigon fell to Communist
forces. North Vietnamese colonel Bui Tin, accepting the sur-
render of South Vietnam later in the day, remarked, "You
have nothing to fear; between Vietnamese there are no victors and no vanquished. Only the Americans have been
defeated." This chilling firsthand account captures the chaos
as both Americans and South Vietnamese fled Saigon while
it fell.*

———□———

The evacuation of Saigon, the whole thing, was called
Operation New Wind or Fresh Wind or Fresh Breeze or something like that. We got to the aircraft carrier *Midway*, and as
soon as we got off the helicopter—since I was a surgical tech,
my hair was always under a cap and it was rather long, about
halfway down my ears—the CO [Commanding Officer], who

was up in the tower, comes down and says, "Get those guys down for haircuts." So right away he gets on us for haircuts.

The *Midway* was our base of operations. Our surgical equipment, all the green crates, never did catch up to us. That's known throughout the military, that they never catch up with you, and the *Midway* didn't have an operating room. This is about April 10 or 11.

We were real close to shore at that time, right off Saigon. We heard that we were taking on a whole bunch of civilians. We would be flying in and out with refugees, with American personnel, with reporters. The Tan Son Nhut airport was being bombed with big rockets. You could see the explosions from the sea. We were flying in and taking on refugees, and they were flying out whatever they could. With the refugees there were worms, women going into labor, TB [tuberculosis] and wounded lying on the choppers because there were a lot of shells coming in. There were a couple dead or dying on the chopper whom we couldn't save. We were landing in Tan Son Nhut. That was our staging point, where everybody was loading.

There were people coming out in boats, half-sinking boats. There were people who had their own airplanes who were flying out. There were all these choppers we had left there; they were using these to fly out, the Vietnamese. The flight deck was so full of choppers that we had to push them overboard because there was no room, we couldn't get our own choppers in. We were flying the big medevac choppers. We had an overload, packing in about twenty-five at a time,

both Vietnamese and American. It was total chaos. The
Purple Heart Trail, the road that came into Saigon from the
paddies west of the city, was so jammed, from the air I
could see columns of people that were at least twenty miles
long. A lot of children crying. Some had clothes they picked
off dead bodies. Most were barefoot. There were oxcarts
and they were hauling what they had. There were wounded
men on both sides of the road with battle dressings on. The
NVA [North Vietnamese Army] was lobbing these rockets all
over the place, they were wiping out civilians . . . There were
piles of wounded on the back of ambulances. They were
dropping the rockets right into the crowds of fleeing people.
There were trucks, buses, anything they could get into.
Saigon was the last stand, the capital, where the American
embassy was.

A lot of American Marines were activated and had put
up a perimeter guard around Tan Son Nhut. The NVA was still
lobbing these rockets in. In fact, when I took off we were also
flying out from the American embassy—a lot of people had
been told to go there instead of Tan Son Nhut. It was really a
mess. These rockets are lobbing in and a C-130 took off full of
people going out to one of the aircraft carriers and it was
blown out of the sky . . . that was all over the runway. There
were corpses, there were burned-out tanks that people had
used to come in, there were pieces of bodies lying in the fields
and on the streets. It was just bananas, total chaos. It was
one mass of humanity being pushed to where people were
being trampled. People screaming, "I want a place on this

chopper!" and not being able to communicate because of the language barrier and because they would not listen.

They were raiding the American Exchange. The image I have is this one guy holding up one of those ten-packs of Kellogg's cereal and he's waving it. They were throwing American money up in the air . . . totally berserk . . . total chaos. We were trying to get the wounded first. They were piled in these old ambulances. The refugees were coming up from the Delta as well as from the North. We were trying to get the wounded out first and a lot of them we just couldn't.

Each time we went in, a bunch of Marines would get out and cover the landing zone as we tried to get the wounded on first, but sometimes they were just overwhelmed. They had orders to shoot if they couldn't maintain order. They shot mostly over the heads. I didn't see any of the Marines shoot any civilians. The Marines set up a defensive perimeter and would return fire at the enemy, but like the rest of the war, you never saw the NVA. The ARVN were running, they were coming in, they were bypassing civilians, shooting civilians, trying to get out first all the time. The best way to describe it was every man for himself. There were pregnant women going into labor right there on the goddamn landing zone. I delivered a baby right on the chopper. And I also delivered two more on the ships. It was just bananas.

We ended up with three thousand civilians aboard the *Midway*. We had taken all of our squadrons off because they had been there for offensive purposes. The civilians all stayed where the squadrons used to be. There were people sleeping on the floors, all over. Of course, they didn't know what a bathroom was. They were packed in, I'll tell you that. So we'd all take turns walking duty and if someone was puking or if someone had diarrhea or worms, we'd treat that.

On April 30, Saigon fell. South Vietnam had fallen.

I have cried my ass off. I don't have any tears left. I first started letting it out in April of 1977. It took two years. I did that because I just couldn't handle being a soldier any- more . . . I got out of the Navy in June of '76, but I still acted like one. I guess I still do in a way. I still sleep with one eye open, you know. And I wake up with bad dreams that I have of taking fire and watching people being mur- dered and being a part of that process. In fact, around this time of year—Christmas time—it gets really heavy for some reason. My wife knows it. Sometimes she feels inadequate because she doesn't know how to deal with that. I get really upset and I have to cry a lot and talk. Once I start it's like for three or four hours. I'm completely exhausted. I cry myself to sleep wherever I am, or I need to go out by myself. People feel inadequate. My wife feels inadequate. I tell her, "There's nothing you can do that can be any more adequate than just to be here." There is no understanding. My mind isn't mature enough. It wasn't then and it isn't now and it's never going to be able to understand murder.

It's a dull pain, you know. Just a whole lot of knowl- edge that I think I've gained, and I think I've grown from it. And I have to deal with that maturity, too, in myself. I grew up real fast. Real fast. It seems like a whole block of my life that I can't account for and I want to find that block because I know it's important. I have a certain pride, too, because I was a damn good medic—I have problems with that. I think a lot of times that it's my fault, and it's not my fault—there is no blame. The actual emotions are a fact. I'm a fresh veteran, I'm really not that old—I'm twenty-five, I'm just out. And there's still a lot of things that I'm real close to in there. A lot of that system I didn't mind. But the people I know say, "Steve, forget it. It's over." The last thing I need is pity.

The last thing I need is someone to feel sorry for me.

My mother told my brother, "Leave Steve alone, he's not the same anymore." This was after my first tour in 'Nam. I guess I was changed and didn't know it. You're the last person to see yourself change. And the fact that you're not going to get any pats on the back, you're not going to get a parade, you're not going to get anything but spit on and misunderstood and blamed—I still feel that sometimes. Maybe I could have done better.

People want me to bury it. I can't bury it. I did learn something and I'm not sure what. But I know it's affected me a whole lot. And I think it's in a good way and I think I've really grown from that, because I don't want to see it happen again and I really care about people. To really try to help people to work through the problems of their own.

CHAPTER FIVE

TIME, CONTINUITY, AND CHANGE: THE LEGACY OF VIETNAM, 1975-PRESENT

"A Maimed Generation"
From **Waiting for an Army to Die: The Tragedy of Agent Orange**
By Fred A. Wilcox
1989

Agent Orange was an herbicide developed by the U.S. military to deny enemy cover and concealment in dense tropical areas such as Vietnam. Agent Orange had its genesis in the 1940s, but it was not fully used and tested until the early 1960s in Vietnam. An estimated 19 million gallons (86 million kiloliters) of Agent Orange (a code name used for the orange band across the drums it was stored in) were sprayed in Vietnamese jungles during the war. In laboratory tests on animals, the herbicide has caused diseases, several of them fatal. Many veterans of the war experienced sicknesses that were unexplained at the time and later were attributed to Agent Orange. This tragedy is just another example of the negative legacy of the war. Together with MIA/POWs, post-war stress disorders, and other unexplained illnesses, Agent Orange proves why the Vietnam War was not only lost, but for many it has not ended.

Author Fred A. Wilcox, a professor at Ithaca College in New York, has been writing and teaching about the Vietnam War for nearly three decades. His 1989 book, Waiting for an Army to Die: The Tragedy of Agent Orange, *was chosen by the American Library Association as one of its most notable books.*

One evening [Vietnam veteran Jerry] Strait is preparing for bed when his mother calls to ask if he has read the newspaper article about "something called Agent Orange." She also wants to know if he recalls having been exposed to herbicides. As he reads, Strait is surprised not only by the statements some veterans are making, but by how much he seems to have forgotten since his return home. Examining a photograph of a C_{123} spraying herbicides, Strait wonders why he has given so little thought to the cysts that spread across his body in Vietnam, clinging to his back, legs, and arms like leeches; or the headaches, dizziness, rashes, and stomach cramps that he and others in his platoon had attributed to the heat. Closing his eyes and leaning back on the couch, Strait remembers the A Shau Valley in 1969. The trees are leafless, rotting, and from a distance appear petrified. The ground is littered with decaying jungle birds; on the surface of a slow-moving stream, clusters of dead fish shimmer like giant buttons. A new arrival "in country" remarks that the scene is spooky, but Strait only shrugs. For him, after several months in the bush, the defoliated area is no more spooky than the corner drugstore in his hometown. Leaving the area, the men walk downstream for thirty minutes before pausing to fill their canteens and helmets with cool water. Some of the men drop in purifying tablets, others do not. After satiating their thirst they splash the remaining water over their necks and faces and then move on.

According to the news article, the VA [Veterans Administration] is offering "Agent Orange examinations" and Strait decides to visit the VA medical clinic. There he is given a four-page questionnaire asking for the time, date, place, and amount of his exposure to Agent Orange. Strait finds the questions peculiar and perplexing. In Vietnam he paid little attention to the spraying, and ten years later it seems ludicrous that he should be asked to remember such details. Although he can vividly recall being in defoliated zones, he did not keep a log of his entry and exit from such areas. "We were fighting a war," says Strait, "not conducting an archeological expedition. It just never really occurred to us that it mattered." Nor was it the Army's policy to tell its troops how recently an area had been sprayed or how much dioxin they might ingest if they drank water or ate food contaminated with Agent Orange. How much was he exposed? That's precisely what Strait wants the VA to tell him.

An hour passes before a physician enters the examining room and, after "poking and prodding" Strait for a few minutes, he explains that he has "received special training in these Agent Orange cases" and can assure the former paratrooper that "Agent Orange and dioxin have never hurt anyone, are not hurting, and never will hurt anyone." After briefly examining Strait's completed questionnaire, the physician informs him that his headaches are "obviously due to war-related stress" and recommends that he pay a visit to the clinic's psychologist. A consultation with the hospital's dietician, says the doctor, will undoubtedly help Strait's skin rash.

Strait is surprised, even angry. What word has he used, he asks himself, that the man doesn't understand? Did he not just explain that he is working at a steady job, does not drink excessively or take drugs, and does not feel he is suffering from "post-Vietnam syndrome." Realizing that his efforts to persuade Strait to see a psychiatrist are futile, the doctor says that he will make an appointment for him to see a dermatologist. Meanwhile, he tells Strait, "My advice to you is that you go home and stop worrying about all this Agent Orange stuff."

During the following weeks the Straits wait anxiously for the results of Jerry's blood and urine analysis; but when weeks, months, and finally a year pass without notice from the clinic, they conclude that they will never hear from the VA again. Two years and three months later, Sandy [Jerry's mother] is astonished to discover a pamphlet in the mail from the VA's Washington headquarters. "We could hardly believe our eyes after all this time," she explains. "On the outside it said, 'WORRIED ABOUT AGENT ORANGE?' And on the inside there is a picture of Max Cleland and he is saying, 'Oh heavens, don't worry about anything like that. Agent Orange never did anybody any real harm.' I guess they think we're pretty dumb, because Jerry and I know that Cleland has not been the VA's director for some time. Why they're still sending his picture around is a mystery to me . . ."

In 1967, Arthur W. Galston, a professor of botany at Yale, tried to warn the U.S. against the continued unbridled use of herbicides in Vietnam. "We are too ignorant of the interplay of forces in ecological problems to know how far-reaching and how lasting will be the changes in ecology brought about by the widespread spraying of herbicides. The changes may include immediate harm to people in sprayed areas . . ."

Galston's warning turned out to be prophetic. Just two years later, reports of birth defects in the offspring of Vietnamese women began appearing in Saigon newspapers, but the U.S. government dismissed the peasants' complaints as communist propaganda, arguing that there was no scientific proof that Agent Orange harmed human beings. Today the government's response, through the Veterans Administration, remains essentially unchanged, in spite of the fact that Vietnam veterans have fathered hundreds and perhaps even thousands of seriously deformed children. At the New York State Temporary Commission on Dioxin Exposure hearings, a veteran testified that "before my son was ten and a half months old he had to have two operations because he had bilateral inguinal hernia, which means his scrotum didn't close, and his intestine was where his scrotum was, and his scrotum was the size of a grapefruit. He also has deformed feet . . . My oldest daughter has a heart murmur and a bad heart. Once she becomes active, you can see her heart beat through her chest as though the chest cavity is not even there, as though you were looking at the heart."

Before Vietnam, said the veteran, he had "never even had an aspirin," but since his return he has been given more than a hundred medications for skin rashes, stomach problems, urine in his blood, and inflamed kidneys. The VA, he testified, has written him off as a "hypochondriac."

"The Birds Still Sang"
From Flashbacks
By Morley Safer
1990

Most people associate the war in Vietnam with jungle warfare and guerrilla fighting tactics. This is, of course, an accurate characterization of the war. However, there was also the military tactic of chemical warfare used by the United States. This strategy created dire consequences not only for American soldiers, but for the Vietnamese as well. The most widely used of these chemical agents was the defoliant Agent Orange. While countless veterans reported effects of exposure to Agent Orange long after the war, the chemical remained part of the Vietnamese landscape, affecting generations of Vietnamese people while dec- imating the Vietnamese jungle. In this scathing excerpt from his book Flashbacks, *former CBS war correspondent Morley Safer revisits the people and land ravaged by years of war.*

—————□—————

3:00 P.M.: We continue the drive north from Quang Tri practically to the old DMZ and then turn off onto an unpaved track, heading for the Trung Son Cemetery. This is as poor a part of Vietnam as I have seen. The houses are made of sticks splattered with mud. The land is a sweeping unproductive plateau. Here and there are a few vegetable gardens; otherwise it is rocky, bony soil where, beyond some stunted trees, nothing else is growing. This is not the Vietnam of the lush deltas and rich coastal plain.

This part of South Vietnam was doused with a monsoon of defoliants. It is impossible for me to tell if this barren plain is the result of nature or the research and development of Dow Chemical and Monsanto, manufacturers of Agent Orange and other useful products. Other firms made Agent Orange as well. Among them, a company with the horrifying name of Thompson-Hayward, Nutrition and Agriculture.

It was chemical warfare pure and simple. Its defenders had the arrogance to maintain that what would kill trees would not hurt people, or American people anyway. We knew it was dirty work from the beginning. An officer confessed it to a friend in 1964, before we were supposed to be using it.

The Vietnamese in these parts tell me that the area around Quang Tri is the most traumatized in all of Vietnam. Beyond the battering it took from the artillery of three armies, the B-52 raids, the regular bombing and strafing of South Vietnamese and American fighter-bombers, there is the legacy of Agent Orange—the poisoned land, the various cancers, the birth defects.

The American servicemen who share the legacy have sued their government. These people have no one to sue. They do not even complain very much. There is no one to complain to. They can only scratch at this unforgiving land for less than enough to eat.

We pass families gathering firewood. Even the smallest among them has an enormous load on his back. All of them, of course, are barefoot on this freezing, wet January day. [Former North Vietnamese soldier Ngugen Ngoc] Hung had asked me earlier what was the most precious thing when I was out on operations in the mud. "Socks," I said, "dry socks." He'd laughed. "We never had to worry about socks."

We drive through the gates of Trung Son Cemetery and stop at the administration building. It is a bare room except for a gold bust of Ho Chi Minh and a few small tables, each one bearing a thick ledger, the kind bookkeepers use. The ledgers contain the names, hometowns, and death dates of ten thousand men and women buried at Trung Son. Hung's face has grown very pale. He is looking for two names, those of his brother and his closest friend. He knows it is extremely unlikely he will find either name, either grave. He has no idea when or where his brother was killed; as for his friend, he'd buried him himself, somewhere along the Laotian border. Still, he hopes that somehow both might have been found and reburied in this Cemetery of Honor.

Hung goes through all the ledgers twice but finds neither name.

There are eighty steps up to the burial ground. The effect of this is to reveal slowly the extent of the place. Not until the final step is reached does one realize that the graves stretch in every direction to the horizon. They are in rows that have been planted in perfectly straight lines. The effect is the same at Arlington or Verdun or St. Laurent-sur-Mer in Normandy. A quarter turn of the head and the eyes catch another perfect row that seems endless. There is the same small blow to the heart, as well. Their youth of course is what does it. The effect on Hung is devastating. He cannot talk for minutes. Then he says, "I have never seen so many in one place. Ten thousand, ten thousand of my family. They were the best sons and daughters of Vietnam."

The effect of his words are as chilling as this place. Years ago I was having a badly needed drink on the terrace of a hotel in Normandy. I had just returned from the cemetery at St. Laurent-sur-Mer, where most of the American casualties suffered at Omaha Beach lay buried. At the next table was a man in his late fifties. He was a veteran of D-Day who made a pilgrimage every year to the cemetery.

"They are like my brothers, you know . . . brothers who never grew old. They were the best sons our country had."

My daughter, who was thirteen at the time, had walked through the cemetery that day with a look of tragic bafflement on her face. She was confronting, perhaps for the first time, or at least in the most powerful way possible, the illogic of death in youth. When she asked "Why?" over and over again, it was not the "Why?" of a child.

The graves at Trung Son are small cement-covered mounds with a Gothic-arched headstone bearing each soldier's name, age, and birthplace. Here and there the markers have fallen over. As we walk along, Hung forces them back into place, firmly but with great tenderness . . . patting each of them when he completes the work. The conversation turns yet again to the B-52 raids. Hung looks up at the overcast sky in this utterly silent place.

"You always knew when the B-52s were coming . . . when the observation and reconnaissance planes would leave, there was silence—except the birds still sang. There was nothing you could do but stare up at the sky and wait. That was it. You knew it was over when the last bomb exploded and you were still alive. In 1972 the B-52s were coming all day, in succession . . . and from Hue to Quang Tri, especially in Quang Tri, you could see nothing at all. The dust was so thick it was as if it was night."

"Did many people desert? Many who could just not take it anymore?"

"In my unit we had some. One soldier, who was terribly brave. One day he came back from an attack and told me about the killing, and that night he had a terrible nightmare about it. The next day he could not eat. He told me that when he looked at the meat he imagined it was human meat, and then he deserted. He was really a very brave man. If he'd stayed, he would have got a medal. But I can't say that I blame him."

Hung's graphic, painful description somehow makes desertion less grievous. On this overcast day, scanning this endless vista of death markers, desertion seems a logical response. Siegfried Sassoon's lovely poem "Dreamers"— "Soldiers are citizens of death's grey land, drawing no dividend from time's tomorrows"—has been running through my head in this place. I think of Bill Baldwin, one of the "vets with a mission," talking about the death of a friend, through sobs he could barely control: ". . . and that morning he was shot by a sniper in the stomach and he was right beside me and it took him fifteen minutes to die. And the shock has never left me. And I can't remember his name . . . and it really bothers me . . . and it's been twenty years . . . and I can't remember his name. I can't remember his name."

The survivors, Bill Baldwin, Nguyen Ngoc Hung, have drawn their dividends, and they are ugly and profitless.

I ask Hung about his friend, how he died.

"What is there to tell? We buried him, or most of him. All I can tell you is that I cried. I cried a lot. When I got back after the war, I went to see his family to tell them the day he died and that we buried him. I went to see them again last year. They will never recover."

There is a tower, a memorial, at the entrance to Trung Son; it bears the legend:

To

Quoc

GHI

CONG

"The Nation Honors Its Glorious Dead"

At the bottom of the inscription is an altar filled to overflowing with ashes. Hung has brought joss sticks with him, the burned offering for the dead. He climbs the steps to the altar and lays the burning sticks among the ashes. His hands drift through the smoke, and he makes a silent prayer. His face is the color of ashes.

As we walk back to the car Hung repeats something he'd said to me in Hanoi, something quite fitting amid these ten thousand graves. Then I had asked him who had won the war. This time I didn't ask; he just spoke, almost thinking out loud.

"At first we thought we won the war . . . but I look at this place and I realize we did not. It was something like fighting with somebody in your house with all the precious furniture around you. And after the stranger leaves, you look at the different things in your house. And they are all broken. The war actually took place in our house. It was a very sad thing. Think about it . . . after all that war, we haven't been able to change you, and you haven't been able to change us."

"War and Accountability"
By Jonathan Schell
From the Nation, May 21, 2001

In excerpts throughout this anthology, we have seen many instances of the atrocities of war committed by both sides. But what happens when the victims are civilians? Furthermore, how do we view the aggressors if those charged with killing civilians unjustly are actually American soldiers? There are countless stories of the malevolence of the Vietcong and how they would do anything in order to kill an American. But little has been said and even less action

*taken about the atrocities committed by our own soldiers. The
following article details an incident in which Vietnamese civilians were killed, not during a battle but during a clandestine
military operation that resulted in the deaths of many
Vietnamese civilians. Author Jonathan Schell, the peace and
disarmament correspondent for the* Nation, *questions the
hypocrisy of the American military and asks the question, How
do we judge these misdeeds, and who is accountable during
these times—the military or the individual?*

—□—

Few things are harder than an honest, voluntary accounting by a
nation of its own crimes. When the crimes are committed by
other nations, people know well how to respond. The pictures—
those of, say, Serbia's recent atrocities in Kosovo shown in the
Western media—are abundant. Investigations are energetic, coverage prompt. The outrage is spontaneous, and the indignation
flows easily. Perhaps judicial proceedings will begin, or "humani-
tarian intervention" will be contemplated, accompanied by a
gratifying debate on the limits of decent outsiders' moral obliga-
tions. Perhaps in time movies will be made showing—and cari-
caturing—their evil and contrasting it with our virtue. Maybe
museums of the horrors will even be founded.

But how different everything becomes when our own
countrymen are the wrongdoers. Investigations move at a
snail's pace—perhaps they take decades, if they occur at all.
Whereas before we seemed to be looking at the events through
a sort of moral telescope, which brought everything near and
into sharp focus, now we seem to look through the telescope's

other end. The figures are small and indistinct. A kind of mental and emotional fog rolls in. Memories dim. The very acts that before inspired prompt anger now become fascinating philosophical puzzles. The psychological torments of the perpetrators move into the foreground, those of the victims into the background. The man firing the gun becomes more of an object of pity than the child at whom the gun was fired.

All of these responses have been on full display in the reaction in this country to the excellent, meticulous report in the *New York Times* by Gregory Vistica on the killing of at least thirteen civilians in February 1969 in the Vietnamese village of Thanh Phong by a Navy SEAL [Sea, Air, Land] team led by Bob Kerrey, now president of the New School University (where, I should state, I am a part-time lecturer) and formerly a senator from Nebraska and presidential candidate. Vistica's original source was Gerhard Klann, a member of Kerrey's team. According to Klann, critical elements of whose account have been corroborated by Vietnamese eyewitnesses independently interviewed, the SEAL team entered the village, known to support the National Liberation Front, at night, to capture its mayor and an NLF representative. Upon arriving at a hut on the outskirts of the village, the team killed five members of a family consisting of two grandparents and their three grandchildren. The SEALs used knives in an attempt to preserve silence. Klann says that when he had trouble killing the grandfather, Kerrey held the man down with his knee while Klann cut his throat. The team, Klann goes on, proceeded to the village, where it ordered about a dozen women and children out of their bunker, lined them up and executed them at close range. Neither the mayor, the NLF representative nor any enemy soldiers or weapons were found.

Kerrey, while admitting that civilians were killed, disputes this account, and his version of events has been supported in a statement signed by the five other members of the seven-man team. All but one of them have declined individual interviews. About the killing at the first hut, the statement of the six is vague: It cryptically says, "At an enemy outpost we used lethal methods to keep our presence from being detected." Kerrey says he did not participate in this killing or know that those killed were two old people and three children. When the team proceeded to the center of the village, the statement says, it received hostile fire, and the civilians were accidentally killed by the American fire in response. Klann's testimony obviously deserves special weight, because it was not in the interest of the testifier and also has been independently confirmed by the Vietnamese eyewitnesses. Although his account is of course sharply at odds with Kerrey's, Kerrey has said, "I'm not going to make this worse by questioning somebody else's memory of it." At the same time, however, he has attacked the *Times* and CBS, which worked on the story with the *Times*, in an interview with the Associated Press. "The Vietnam government likes to routinely say how terrible Americans were," he said. "The *Times* and CBS are now collaborating in that effort." Kerrey's other responses have likewise been uncertain and changeable. He has been, by turns, confessional, apologetic, tormented, defensive, anguished, irritable, forgetful and contrite.

Kerrey has been an uncommonly thoughtful, constructive, independent public figure. Volunteering to serve his country in what he believed was a just war, he found himself instead in a slaughterhouse devoid of reason. (Upon returning to the United States, he became a fervent opponent of the war.) He has flatly stated, for instance, "We were instructed not to take prisoners." If so, he was instructed to commit war crimes—doubly, if the potential "prisoners" were civilians. According to the US military adviser on the scene, David Marion, the policy of the local Vietnamese district chief toward civilians in the area was, "If you are my friend, you will do fine. You support me and the government of Vietnam, we get along OK. You do not, you're Vietcong, you die." Marion, who observed the results of these policies firsthand, confirmed to Vistica that in practice, "Those were the rules."

I can testify from my experience in Vietnam as a reporter in 1967 that the rules in other parts of the country were the same. In the northern provinces of South Vietnam, villagers in "free-fire zones" were warned that if they supported the NLF their villages would be bombed, and I witnessed the execution and the results of this policy throughout Quang Ngai and Quang Tri provinces. The policy, which contravened the laws of war forbidding the deliberate targeting of civilians, was nowhere written down in government documents, but it was announced in millions of leaflets showered from planes on Vietnamese villages, and it was carried out. One leaflet, for example, read, "Many hamlets have been destroyed because these villages harbored the Vietcong. The hamlets of

Hai Mon, Hai Tan, Sa Binh, Tan Binh, and many others have been destroyed because these villages harbored the Vietcong. We will not hesitate to destroy every hamlet that helps the Vietcong . . . "

These de facto policies obviously placed an extraordinary oral burden on the young men sent to carry them out. However, the struggles of Bob Kerrey to come to terms personally with his experience are of secondary importance. What is of first importance is exactly what was done that day, what the response of the American public and government to this will be, and whether anyone is to be held accountable. A serious war crime has been credibly alleged. Did it happen? Is anyone responsible? Will they be held responsible?

So far, it looks as if, through a series of subterfuges and evasions, there will be neither an adequate investigation nor any accountability. In its editorial, the *Times* commented: "With the emergence of this story, Mr. Kerrey's career has entered a new phase of public assessment." Even this muffled admonition, however, was too much for Mark Shields of the *NewsHour With Jim Lehrer*, who called the editorial "an act of moral arrogance rarely seen." Kerrey, he explained, had not ducked service in Vietnam, as so many others had done, and had never bragged about that service. But the question, of course, is not whether Kerrey was a coward or a braggart—he obviously was neither—but whether on February 24, 1969, he twice ordered the massacre of civilians—first at the hut, second in the village. The debate so far has concentrated on whether there was hostile fire before the killings in the center of the village, as if the unit's entire conduct could be excused by it. However, that question has no bearing on the horrifying scene at the hut, which remains without explanation. If the nation should not engage in any reassessment of Kerrey, should it at least try to find out, by means of a Pentagon investigation, what happened that night? Three senators who served in Vietnam and were decorated for their valor—John Kerry, Max Cleland and Chuck Hagel—think not, as they said on ABC's *This Week*. (A fourth, John McCain, wanted to leave the decision up to the Pentagon.)

Their reasons are noteworthy. You have to take into account the special circumstance into which the war placed Kerrey, the senators said. The SEALs' mission "was to take out the civilian infrastructures," John Kerry observed. The Phoenix program, whose objective was "assassination" of NLF leaders, was in operation, he added. It was the nature of war that civilians "suffer the most," Hagel said. Civilians had been killed in the tens of thousands, Kerry continued, by the fire-bombing of Dresden and at Hiroshima and Nagasaki. In short, they cleared the individual by condemning the war. As Kerry said, if Bob Kerrey was to be judged, then "you'd have to investigate the whole war."

Some have suggested that the United States has anguished long enough over the Vietnam War and that it's long past time to put it behind us. The debate over Thanh Phong, however, occurs in a new context. Today, nations all over the world—South Africa, Chile, Argentina, Poland, the Czech Republic, Serbia, Rwanda, to name just a few—have been struggling to come to terms with crimes committed in their recent past. In some countries, judicial proceedings are under way. In others, truth commissions, offering amnesty in exchange for full confession, have been founded. Elsewhere, lustration—laws preventing wrongdoers of the past from holding office—has been the recourse. Western countries have been liberal with their advice. "International civil society" has added its voice. Hundreds of academic conferences have been held. In still other cases, international tribunals have been created at The Hague to bring committers of crimes against humanity to justice. Special tribunals are in operation to prosecute the perpetrators of the genocide in Rwanda and the ethnic cleansing of Kosovo by Serbia. The United States is among many countries that have sought the extradition of the former president of Serbia, Slobodan Milosevic, and others to face justice at The Hague. More important, thirty countries have ratified an agreement to establish a permanent international criminal court. Taken in their entirety, these efforts amount to a sort of movement, in the wake of the terrible violence of the twentieth century, to create a bare minimum of accountability for the worst crimes in the twenty-first.

The reactions of journalists and senators on news programs in the United States to the Thanh Phong massacre will not decide the outcome of these efforts. But if as a nation the United States—the self-styled "world's only superpower"—cannot investigate, cannot condemn, cannot assign responsibility for the killing of the women and children of Thanh Phong, then state-licensed murderers everywhere will take heart and those who are seeking to bring them to justice will be discouraged. The United States cannot condemn in others what it covers up when committed by its own. The movement for justice will continue, but the voice of the United States will be discredited. We'll be missing in action.

"The Lessons of Vietnam" From In Retrospect
By Robert S. McNamara with Brian VanDeMark
1995

After more than twenty-five years out of the public eye, former defense secretary Robert McNamara offers us his unique perspective of the Vietnam conflict in his memoir, In Retrospect. *Many still consider McNamara to be the architect of the war and a man who, for seven years, shadowed Presidents Kennedy and Johnson. McNamara says that the two administrations he served made decisions that were "terribly wrong," not because they lacked values and intentions but because they lacked "judgement and capabilities." The knowledge of retrospection is very keen, and it is important to investigate the causes and the reasons why many decisions were made and how these mistakes can be avoided by future generations.*

————□————

My involvement with Vietnam ended the day after I left the East Room [of the White House]. The war, of course, went on for another seven years. By the time the United States finally left South Vietnam in 1973, we had lost over 58,000 men and women; our economy had been damaged by years of heavy and

improperly financed war spending; and the political unity of
our society had been shattered, not to be restored for decades.

Were such high costs justified?

Dean Rusk, Walt Rostow, Lee Kwan Yew, and many
other neopoliticians across the globe to this day answer yes.
They conclude that without U.S. intervention in Vietnam,
Communist hegemony—both Soviet and Chinese—would have
spread farther through South and East Asia to include control
of Indonesia, Thailand, and possibly India. Some would go further and say that the USSR would have been led to take
greater risks to extend its influence elsewhere in the world,
particularly in the Middle East, where it might well have
sought control of the oil-producing nations. They might be cor-
rect, but I seriously question such judgments.

When the archives of the former Soviet Union, China, and
Vietnam are opened to scholars, we will know more about those
countries' intentions, but even without such knowledge we know
that the danger of Communist aggression during the four
decades of the Cold War was real and substantial. Although during the 1950s, 1960s, 1970s, and 1980s the West often misper-
ceived, and therefore exaggerated, the power of the East and its
ability to project that power, to have failed to defend ourselves
against the threat would have been foolhardy and irresponsible.

That said, today I question whether either Soviet or
Chinese behavior and influence in the 1970s and 1980s would
have been materially different had the United States not
entered the war in Indochina or had we withdrawn from
Vietnam in the early or mid-1960s. By then it should have
become apparent that the two conditions underlying President

Kennedy's decision to send military advisers to South Vietnam were not being met and, indeed, could not be met: political stability did not exist and was unlikely ever to be achieved; and the South Vietnamese, even with our training assistance and logistical support, were incapable of defending themselves.

Given these facts—and they are facts—I believe we could and should have withdrawn from South Vietnam either in late 1963 amid the turmoil following Diem's assassination or in late 1964 or early 1965 in the face of increasing political and military weakness in South Vietnam.

I do not believe that U.S. withdrawal at any of these junctures, if properly explained to the American people and to the world, would have led West Europeans to question our support for NATO [North Atlantic Treaty Organization] and, through it, our guarantee of their security. Nor do I believe that Japan would have viewed our security treaties as any less credible. On the contrary, it is possible we would have improved our credibility by withdrawing from Vietnam and saving our strength for more defensible stands elsewhere . . .

I want to add a final word on Vietnam.

Let me be simple and direct—I want to be clearly understood: the United States of America fought in Vietnam for eight years for what it believed to be good and honest reasons. By such action, administrations of both parties sought to protect our security, prevent the spread of totalitarian Communism, and promote individual freedom and political democracy. The Kennedy, Johnson, and Nixon administrations made their decisions and by those decisions demanded sacrifices and, yes, inflicted terrible suffering in light of those goals and values.

Their hindsight was better than their foresight. The adage goes down the corridors of time, applying to many individuals, in many situations, in many ages. People are human; they are fallible. I concede with painful candor and a heavy heart that the adage applies to me and to my generation of American leadership regarding Vietnam. Although we sought to do the right thing—and believed we were doing the right thing—in my judgment, hindsight proves us wrong. We both overestimated the effect of South Vietnam's loss on the security of the West and failed to adhere to the fundamental principle that, in the final analysis, if the South Vietnamese were to be saved, they had to win the war themselves. Straying from this central truth, we built a progressively more massive effort on an inherently unstable foundation. External military force cannot substitute for the political order and stability that must be forged by a people for themselves.

In the end, we must confront the fate of those Americans who served in Vietnam and never returned. Does the unwisdom of our intervention nullify their effort and their loss? I think not. They did not make the decisions. They answered their nation's call to service. They went in harm's way on its behalf. And they gave their lives for their country and its ideals. That our effort in Vietnam proved unwise does not make their sacrifice less noble. It endures for all to see. Let us learn from their sacrifice and, by doing so, validate and honor it.

Each human being lives with unrealized dreams and unfulfilled objectives. Certainly I have. But now, as a century of bloody conflict comes to a close, we have an opportunity to view the future with new hope: The Cold War has ended. We have the lessons of Vietnam before us—they can be learned and applied. We should see more clearly the dangers of a world armed with thousands of nuclear weapons, and we can take steps to avoid nuclear catastrophe. We have a better understanding of the potential—and limitations—of multilateral institutions for minimizing and alleviating disputes within and among nations. Do we not have reason, therefore, to believe that the twenty-first century, while not a century of tranquility, need not witness the killing of another 160 million people by war? Surely that must be not only our hope, not only our dream, but our steadfast objective. Some may consider such a statement so naive, so simplistic, and so idealistic as to be quixotic. But as human beings, citizens of a great nation with the power to influence events in the world, can we be at peace with ourselves if we strive for less?

"Her Parents' Legacy"
By Wendy Loughlin
From the Vietnam Reader
2002

Located between the Washington Monument and the Lincoln Memorial on the Mall in Washington, D.C., the dramatic and somber Vietnam Veterans Memorial was dedicated in November 1982. The V-shaped memorial consists of two 250-foot (76-meter) walls of polished black granite sloping to the ground from an apex of 10 feet (3 m). The walls are inscribed with the names of the more than 58,000 U.S. men and women

who were killed or declared missing in action during the
Vietnam War.

The following article details a young woman's visit to
the memorial. The author wrestles with the ghost of Vietnam
as her generation, younger and far removed from the turbulent
1960s, comes to terms with the legacy of a terrible and unjus-
tified war that has bloodied the hands of a proud country.

———□———

It was the Saturday after Veteran's Day in Washington, D.C.,
and at least 200 people had gathered near the edge of the
Mall to file past the polished granite wall of the Vietnam
Veterans Memorial. The black expanse was morbidly beautiful
in the afternoon sun, reflecting the faces of the visitors who
stood before it. I walked the length of the monument, part of a
crowd as silent as the stone.

Mementos adorned the Wall all along its base: poems,
flowers, American flags. A little girl skipped forward to look
at an Army shirt that lay folded on the ground. "Mom, what's
this all about?" she asked. Her mother was crying too hard
to respond.

The Wall slopes upward toward the middle to represent
the steady increase of deaths that marked the progression of the
Vietnam War. At the place where the slab reaches its highest
level, I saw a piece of white cardboard propped against the
stone. A photograph of a young man in fatigues, and that man's
obituary, were pasted to the bottom of the sign. Written above,
a message: "After 22 years, I'm going to finally say good-bye."

Twenty-two years spans almost the entire length of my
life. I cannot remember this war that ended when I was a

child. The body bags, the evening news, the protests, the grief—it is all remote to me, all a piece of history, like the Great Depression or the New Frontier.

And yet, as I looked at the 58,000 names etched on that wall, as I witnessed the tears and the emotions of the people who gathered there, I felt a kind of link to this war that I do not feel for any other element of history that precedes my birth. There are pictures of my mother, as young as I am today, with peace symbols painted on her cheeks; there are my father's dog tags, hidden in his dresser drawer. I do not know the man and the woman they were back then, but somehow, that man and that woman are a part of me. And if their generation was shaped and changed by the Vietnam War, my generation continues to feel the effects of that war, some 25 years after its finish.

For my generation, Vietnam touches us in fragments of emotion rather than overwhelming us with one intense feeling. It comes to us through songs, pictures, film footage. And, as we look back at it through our parents' eyes, it comes to us as a memory that, although we never owned it, is nonetheless striking and vivid. So, like our parents, we regard that time with confusion. We see our fathers, sent to fight in a war they did not understand; we see the loss of young lives, which in retrospect seem squandered. But we also see a movement that rocked administrations and made people listen. And we realize that our parents were players in a process that brought about change and gave power to the young.

Still, the legacy of that war is often difficult for my generation to decipher, and difficult to accept. Laurie Liddell, a 23-year-old student in public policy, said that, thinking about Vietnam, she feels a sense of bitterness. "I think our parents, because of their experience with that war, instilled in us a great feeling of distrust and corruption," she said. "We look at our government with suspicious eyes. We even look at each other that way."

Liddell also believes that much of the so-called apathy of the younger generation stems in part from the memory of Vietnam. Many children of the baby boomers react to their parents' past with indecisiveness. "We are a bunch of moderates," she said of her generation. "We are afraid to be left-wing, but unwilling to be conservative. That's why we are the generation X. The Vietnam era left us confused."

But not all young people feel that way. Elizabeth Madigan, a 24-year-old paralegal in New York City, said she thinks the Vietnam legacy has a lot to do with freedom. "Our parents felt they had the right to stand up to their government, to question the way things were," she said. "I think that has, in turn, given us a lot more freedom in our time, despite some of the pessimism and negativity we may have to face."

Still, my generation, born and raised in post-Vietnam America, has always known that pessimism. It is hard for us to comprehend the hope and optimism of the "American Dream" idea that surrounded our parents' childhood—a notion that was later contradicted by the war in Vietnam. My father told me of growing up in the idyllic 1950s, a time marked by a nationalistic adoration of the United States that had been fostered and nourished in the afterglow of World War II. "I just can't explain to you what it was like then," he told me, knowing that, to my generation, such unquestioning faith in country and government is an archaic idea.

Still, it was partly the serenity of the Eisenhower years that made the coming turbulence so hard to bear. "We grew up believing we were the best, we took it for granted," my father said. "All that changed with Vietnam." In retrospect, the war appears as the starting point for a slow disputation of those ideals set forth at the end of World War II. And the whole period leading up to Vietnam seems like a steady flow into the turbulent 1960s. As my father observed, "1945 kicked us into the future—into the brick wall of Vietnam."

Part of the betrayal of Vietnam lay in a discrepancy, for the baby boomers, between the things they had been taught and believed in as children and the horrible, often unbeliev- able things that came with the war. My father said that, despite his initial doubts about Vietnam, he still wanted to serve. "I loved my country, and it was the right thing to do," he said. "I was patriotic, I believed in America. It was just so hard to accept that what we were doing over there might be wrong. So I did my duty."

I do not think the Vietnam War shattered the American Dream, but I do believe it did a lot to alter that concept, and to change the self-image of America. Now, more than 35 years after the war began, I can only imagine the kind of patriotism that made many young men willing to go to Vietnam. The notion of fighting a hard and fearful war for duty and honor seems almost dated and strange, though

I know that part of me mourns those lost convictions. Maybe it's because our parents paid such a high price for those beliefs that my generation has strayed from them. We do not want that kind of betrayal, that kind of mental injury, to infest our youth the way it did theirs. We are unwilling. That unwillingness is one of the things our parents taught us.

My mother remembered the war as it looked to her then. She was a teenager, listening to the chants of protesters and watching the death toll mount on her television screen. "I was terrified," she remembered. "So much was out of our control. But at the same time, we had power. We were going to make a change. It was a revolution." I understand her meaning now, though I don't believe the movements of the 1960s truly brought a revolution. And I know that she must not believe that, either.

I think there is a certain sadness among the baby boomers today when they realize that the ideals of their "Woodstock Nation" have not come to pass. My generation senses that. Referring to the Janis Joplin song "Me and Bobby McGee," Elizabeth Madigan said, "That line: 'Freedom's just another word for nothing left to lose'—well, I think that came back to slap them in the face." And Laurie Liddell noted that the boomers' authority status within the system they once hated must be hard for them to accept. "They thought it was a revolution, but where did it take them? They said, 'Don't trust anyone over 30.' Well, 30 has come and gone for them, and I don't think they know what to do now."

Still, my mother thinks a lot that is good can be attributed to the era of the counterculture. "I think we gave our children the power to ask why, to look before they leap," she said. "We want informed choices for our children. We don't want them to have to take everything for granted, like we did, and then watch it backfire."

So we took nothing for granted, and perhaps we are grateful for the heightened awareness brought about by our parents' coming of age in a deeply divided nation. But today, when negative journalism is the cornerstone of society and the president's sexual behavior warrants more coverage than his legislative activities, we may long for some of the lost innocence and hope of our parents' youth. My generation knows no John Kennedys.

The war itself remains the sticking point for most Americans today, regardless of generation. And although I cannot personally remember the feeling of that time—I did not experience the draft, or the loss of a brother, husband, father or son—still, I have come to understand how that war changed our society and, as a result, our lives. If analysis of the war is full of guesses, confusion and half-truths, this fact remains clearly intact.

So many questions remain unanswered. As young now as our parents were then, there are those in my generation who are no less desperate to find the answers. It's hard to say why Vietnam remains such a forceful presence in our lives. But I think we know that, good or bad, obvious or subtle, we learn something from that time, and we carry it with us.

This is one of the reasons why so many young Americans today visit the Wall. Standing before the memorial, we face 58,000 names—lives cut short, possibilities ended, senseless-ness etched in stone. But the polished granite wall presents us with another image as well—that of our own faces, reflected across the names. We know the Vietnam era left our nation with a void of hope. Perhaps we need to fill that void with ourselves.

In the end, the emotional connection between my gen-eration and the Vietnam War, like the Wall itself, represents a memorial to the trials of that time. We cannot, on our own, remember the war. But we have been raised, taught, and influenced by a generation for whom that war was the single most defining element of their coming of age. Our parents give us many things, not the least of which are their memories.

TIMELINE

1954 —— French forces leave Vietnam following the Indochina War; Geneva Accords divide Vietnam at the 17th parallel until elections are held.

1955 —— South Vietnam, supported by the United States, opts out of proposed elections.

1957 —— Communist forces begin moving into South Vietnam.

1959 —— Communist forces begin moving weapons and supplies south along the Ho Chi Minh Trail.

1960 —— The NLF is formed in South Vietnam; John F. Kennedy is elected president.

1961 —— Vice President Lyndon Johnson visits South Vietnam.

1962 —— U.S. forces begin using Agent Orange in Vietnam.

1963 —— President John F. Kennedy is assassinated; South Vietnamese president Diem is assassinated.

1964 —— The Gulf of Tonkin incident occurs in early August. The Tonkin Gulf Resolution passes through Congress on August 7 and authorizes President Johnson to use any means necessary to prevent further aggression.

1965 —— The first American combat troops arrive in Danang, South Vietnam; heavy fighting in the Ia Drang Valley; American troops in Vietnam reach 200,000 by the end of the year.

1966 —— American B-52s run heavy bombing raids over North Vietnam; the antiwar movement begins to gain momentum on college campuses across the United States.

1968 ——— The Tet Offensive begins January 31; battle for Hue in February; My Lai massacre occurs March 16; President Johnson announces he will not run for reelection; Martin Luther King Jr. is assassinated; Robert Kennedy is assassinated; Democratic National Convention is held in Chicago; Richard Nixon is elected president; President Nixon begins bombing of Cambodia; Ho Chi Minh dies; massive antiwar demonstration takes place in Washington, D.C.

1970 ——— Kent State massacre; number of U.S. troops in Vietnam down to 280,000; Pentagon Papers are published; President Nixon visits China.

1972 ——— Secret peace talks are held between the United States and North Vietnam; break-in occurs at the Watergate Hotel in Washington, D.C.; Secretary of State Henry Kissinger announces "Peace is at hand"; Nixon wins reelection.

1973 ——— Cease-fire agreement is signed in Paris by Kissinger and Le Duc Tho; the two are awarded the Nobel Peace Prize. Kissinger accepts the award; Tho declines, citing that peace has not been reached in Vietnam.

1974 ——— War is renewed; reports of effects of herbicides in Vietnam are released; North Vietnam seizes Mekong Delta region; Nixon resigns from office following the Watergate scandal.

1975 ——— Hue and Saigon fall to Communists; Vietnam is reunited under Communist rule.

1982 ——— Vietnam War Memorial is dedicated in Washington, D.C.

FOR MORE INFORMATION

Kent State May 4 Center
P.O. Box 3313
Kent, OH 44240
Web site: http://www.may4.org

The National Vietnam War Museum (Florida)
3400 North Tanner Road
Orlando, FL 32826
(407) 273-0201
Web site: http://www.nvwm.org/contact.html

The National Vietnam War Museum (Texas)
P.O. Box 146
Mineral Wells, TX 76068-0146
Web site: http://www.nationalvnwarmuseum.org

United States Air Force Museum
1100 Spaatz Street
Wright-Patterson AFB, OH 45433
(937) 255-3286
Web site: http://www.wpafb.af.mil/museum/index.htm

Vietnam Veterans Memorial
900 Ohio Drive SW
Washington, DC 20242
(202) 426-6841
Web site: http://www.nps.gov/vive/home.htm

Web Sites

Due to the changing nature of Internet links, the Rosen Publishing Group, Inc., has developed an online list of Web sites related to the subject of this book. This site is updated regularly. Please use this link to access the list:

http://www.rosenlinks.com/canf/viwa

FOR FURTHER READING

Edelman, Bernard, ed. *Dear America: Letters Home from Vietnam*. New York: W. W. Norton & Company, 2002.

Halberstam, David. *The Making of a Quagmire*. New York: McGraw-Hill, 1987.

Herr, Michael. *Dispatches*. New York: Alfred A. Knopf, 1977.

Karnow, Stanley. *Vietnam: A History*. New York: Penguin, 1997.

Moore, Lt. Gen. Harold G., and Joseph Galloway. *We Were Soldiers Once . . . and Young*. New York: Random House, 1992.

Myers, Walter Dean. *Fallen Angels*. New York: Scholastic, 2003.

O'Brien, Tim. *The Things They Carried: A Work of Fiction.* New York: Broadway Books, 1999.

O'Nan, Stewart, ed. *Vietnam: A Reader*. New York: Anchor, 1998.

Wallace, Terry. *Bloods: An Oral History of the Vietnam War by Black Veterans*. New York: Ballantine Books, 1989.

White, Ellen Emerson. *The Road Home*. New York: Scholastic, 1995.

ANNOTATED BIBLIOGRAPHY

Andrade, Dale, and Kenneth Conboy. "The Secret Side of the Tonkin Gulf Incident." *Naval History*, August 1999. Reprinted from *Naval History* with permission. Copyright © (1999) U.S. Naval Institute.

Authors Conboy and Andrade, a Vietnam War historian with the U.S. Army Center of Military History, uncover the truth behind the Tonkin Gulf incident and President Johnson's justification for the Vietnam War.

Bigart, Homer. "Vietnam Victory Remote Despite U.S. Aid to Diem." *The New York Times*, July 25, 1962. Copyright © 1962 by New York Times Co. Reprinted with permission.

One of America's most distinguished war correspondents, Bigart assesses the Vietnam situation more than two years before the Tonkin Gulf Resolution. The author insists that victory in Vietnam cannot be accomplished.

Cronkite, Walter. "We Are Mired in a Stalemate . . ." *Reporting Vietnam, Part One*. New York: Library Classics of the United States, 1998.

CBS anchorman Walter Cronkite, whose nightly broadcasts brought the Vietnam War into living rooms around the country, assesses the war in early 1968.

"The Fall of Saigon, April, 1975." The Gale Group. Retrieved June 2003 (http://galenet.galegroup.com/servlet/Histrc/). Copyright © 1975, Gale Group. Reprinted with permission of the Gale Group.

Written by an unidentified author, this firsthand account captures the chaos as refugees flee Saigon while the city falls to the North Vietnamese.

Fallows, James. "What Did You Do in the Class War, Daddy?" the *Washington Monthly*, October 1975. Reprinted with permission from the *Washington Monthly*. Copyright by Washington Monthly Publishing, LLC, 733 15th St. NW, Suite 520, Washington, DC, 20005. (202) 393-5155. Web site: http://www.washingtonmonthly.com.

Several years after avoiding the draft, Fallows revisits the summer he and his friends opted out of a war they did not believe in. Years later, the author is haunted by the memory of those men who were less well-off and who were drafted into a war no one understood.

Halberstam, David. "An Endless, Relentless War." *The Making of a Quagmire: America and Vietnam During the Kennedy Era.* New York: McGraw-Hill, 1987. Copyright © 1987 David Halberstam. Reprinted with permission.

A Pulitzer Prize–winning account of American escalation into the Vietnam conflict. Halberstam dissects the political and moral implications of the situation in Vietnam.

Herr, Michael. "Breathing In." *Dispatches*. New York: Alfred A. Knopf, 1977.

The definitive firsthand account of the Vietnam War from a journalist who captured the madness of war on the front lines.

Johnson, Lyndon B. "The Tonkin Gulf Incident Address." August 8, 1964. Retrieved May 2003 (http://www. historicaldocuments.com).

Citing aggressions by the North Vietnamese, President Johnson addresses Congress days before escalating the Vietnam conflict into a full-blown war.

Kennedy, John F. "A Letter from President Kennedy to
President Ngo Dinh Diem." December 14, 1961. Retrieved
May 2003 (http://www.historicaldocuments.com).
President Kennedy pledges to stand with the South
Vietnamese and stand down the Communist threat haunting
Southeast Asia.

Kerry, John. "Vietnam Veterans Against the War Statement."
Retrieved June 2003 (http://www.historicaldocuments.com).
Kerry, a decorated veteran, returns to the United States
and finds an audience in the United States Senate.
Pointing to the atrocities he witnessed while in
Vietnam, Kerry pleads with the Senate to pull troops
from an unjustified war.

Kutler, Stanley I. *Abuse of Power*. New York: the Free Press,
1997. Reprinted with the permission of the Free Press,
a division of Simon & Schuster Adult Publishing Group,
from *Abuse of Power: The New Nixon Tapes* by Stanley I.
Kutler. Copyright © 1997 by Stanley I. Kutler. All rights
reserved.
Historian Stanley Kutler brings to light thousands of
hours of conversations recorded between President Nixon
and his staff. The dialogue gives an intimate understanding of the mentality of the administration behind the
Vietnam War and the Watergate scandal.

Lerner, Steve. "A Visit to Chicago: Blood, Sweat, and Tears." *The
Village Voice*, September 5, 1968.
The country's premier alternative newspaper covers the
chaos of the 1968 Democratic National Convention at the
height of the anti-war movement in the United States.

Loughlin, Wendy. "Her Parents' Legacy." *The Vietnam Reader.* New York: Ibooks, Inc., 2002. This article is reproduced from *Vietnam Magazine* with the permission of PRIMEDIA Special Interest Publications (History Group), copyright *Vietnam Magazine.*
A young author visits the Vietnam Memorial and struggles with the ghosts of the Vietnam generation.

Luce, Don. "Tell Your Friends That We're People." *The Pentagon Papers, Vol. 5.* New York: Beacon Press, 1972.
An accomplished war correspondent, Luce visits with those lost in the fog of war—the peasant population of Vietnam.

McNamara, Robert S., with Brian VanDeMark. "The Lessons of Vietnam." *In Retrospect: The Tragedy and Lessons of Vietnam.* New York: Times Books, 1995. Copyright © 1995 by Robert S. McNamara. Used by permission of Times Books, a division of Random House, Inc.
Through his memoirs, the former defense secretary offers an unprecedented account of the Vietnam War.

Moore, Lt. Gen. Harold G., and Joseph Galloway. "The Secretary of the Army Regrets . . . " *We Were Soldiers Once . . . and Young.* New York: Random House, 1992. Copyright © 1992 by Lt. General H. G. Moore and Joseph L. Galloway. Used by permission of Random House, Inc.
Shocking firsthand account of when Lt. Gen. Harold Moore, journalist Joseph Galloway, and 450 marines found themselves surrounded by more than 2,000 Vietcong guerrillas in the Ia Drang Valley.

Nixon, Richard M. "Peace with Honor." January 23, 1973. Retrieved June 2003 (http://www. historicaldocuments.com).

President Nixon addresses the nation to explain that the
United States has attained "peace with honor" and the war
will soon be at an end. The war in Vietnam would, in fact,
continue for two more years.

Pekkanen, John. "A Boy Who Was Just 'There Watching It and
Making Up His Mind.'" *Life*, May 15, 1970. Copyright ©
1970 Time Inc. Reprinted by permission.
Life visits the aftermath of the massacre at Kent State with
an intimate portrait of one student slain on May 4, 1970.

"Pentagon's Statistics Underscore Intensity of Cambodia
Bombing." *The New York Times*, June 22, 1973. Copyright ©
1973 by New York Times Co. Reprinted with permission
A staggering hard news account of the massive bombing
campaign over Cambodia intended to disrupt North
Vietnamese troop and supply movement along the Ho Chi
Minh Trail.

Pisor, Robert. "The Tet Offensive." *The End of the Line: The
Siege of Khe Sanh*. New York: Norton, 1982. Copyright ©
1982 by Robert Pisor. Used by permission of W. W.
Norton & Company, Inc.
War correspondent Pisor captures the horror at Khe Sanh
when American forces found themselves surrounded by
the North Vietnamese, outnumbered nearly seven to one.
The definitive book on one of the most important
episodes in the Vietnam War.

Safer, Morley. "The Birds Still Sang." *Flashbacks*. New York:
Random House, 1990. Copyright © 1990 by Morley
Safer. Used by permission of Random House, Inc.
A young war correspondent in Vietnam during the war,

Safer returns to Vietnam in the 1980s, searching for
answers that have haunted his generation.

Schell, Jonathan. "War and Accountability." *The Nation*, May 21,
2001, Vol. 272, Issue 20. Reprinted with permission from
the May 3, 2001, issue of the *Nation*. For subscription information, call 1-800-333-8536. Portions of each week's *Nation*
magazine can be accessed at http://www.thenation.com.
Citing the massacre at Thanh Phong, where innocent civilians were slaughtered by U.S. Marines, the author searches
for accountability for the atrocities committed in Vietnam
by American soldiers.

Sheehan, Neil, et al., eds. *The Pentagon Papers as Published by
the New York Times*. New York: Bantam Books, 1971.
Award-winning journalist Sheehan documents the struggle
between the *New York Times* and the federal government,
which intended to block the newspaper's publishing of the
Pentagon Papers. A landmark decision by the Supreme
Court would end the matter in favor of the *Times*.

Smith, Jack P. "Death in the Ia Drang Valley." *The Saturday
Evening Post*, January 28, 1967.
The author captures the horror of a massive firefight, where
American GIs find themselves in a massacre, surrounded by
an enemy they cannot see.

U.S. State Department. "Aggression from the North."
February 27, 1965. Retrieved May 2003 (http://
www.historicaldocuments.com).
This white paper sets out a detailed justification for
escalating the conflict in Vietnam.

Van Dyke, Jon M. "Infiltration: The Long Journey South."
North Vietnam's Strategy for Survival. Palo Alto, CA:
Pacific Books, 1972.
The author investigates the United States' massive
bombing campaign over North Vietnam and how the
North Vietnamese adapted and continued to infiltrate
South Vietnam.

Wilcox, Fred A. "A Maimed Generation." *Waiting for an Army
to Die: The Tragedy of Agent Orange*. New York: Random
House, 1989. Copyright © 1989 Fred Wilcox. Used by
permission of Random House, Inc.
Chronicles one of the darkest episodes in American
history—the creation, implementation, and effects of
Agent Orange.

INDEX

About the Editor

Gilbert Morales Jr. is an adjunct professor with the City University of New York and currently teaches at John Jay College of Criminal Justice and Hunter College. A native New Yorker, he is also involved in developing literacy programs for out-of-school high school youths.

Cover © Bettmann/Corbis

Designer: Tom Forget; Series Editor: Charles Hofer